PERSONAL RESPONSIBILITY AND THE LAW OF NATIONS

by

ELIZABETH THORNEYCROFT M.A. (OXON)

of the Inner Temple Barrister-at-Law

Member of the Bar of British Columbia

Springer-Science+Business Media, B.V. / 1961

Originally published by Martinus Nijhoff, The Hague, Netherlands in 1961
Softcover reprint of the hardcover 1st edition 1961

ISBN 978-94-017-5713-3
DOI 10.1007/978-94-017-6054-6
ISBN 978-94-017-6054-6 (eBook)

This book is dedicated to the memory of my father

Acknowledgements

I am indebted to many people of many nationalities and professions for their advice and comments on the several drafts of this book. I cannot mention them all, but I must express my gratitude to two of them. First I thank Mr. Henry Usborne of Great Britain who was sufficiently impressed by the central idea of the first draft to have it stencilled and distributed for comment. From these comments I gathered a useful harvest, and as a result attracted the interest of Dr. Georges Kaeckenbeeck of Belgium to whom I owe the greatest debt of all. On his advice and with the help of his criticism and encouragement I rewrote the book twice, stripping it of matter not strictly germane to its principal theme and guarding as far as possible against the misconceptions to which earlier drafts had given rise in the minds of critics. If the idea now published turns out to be of value much credit is due to him, but the responsibility is mine alone.

Acknowledgement is also due to the Editor of the *International Law Review* (Sottile - Geneva) for permission to make use of passages from my article "International Delinquency" published in that review (1959, 3).

ELIZABETH THORNEYCROFT

1

The changing character of sovereignty

Until this century public international law has been regarded as the law governing the relations between sovereign states. Only states, it was constantly said in the text books, could have rights under international law, and as a corollary, only states could be directly bound by its obligations. This was natural since the European system was designed by the early writers to regulate the relations of sovereign kings. Its authority was moral authority, and it owed its origin to an appeal to the consciences and to the personal honour of Monarchs.

The sovereign person of modern international law is not however an individual, but a collective entity – the nation state. Its sovereign authority is not exercised by a monarch but by many men, Presidents, Prime Ministers, Foreign Ministers, Members of the Cabinet, Senators and Parliamentarians – only rarely Kings – participate in international decisions.

The idea of making men personally responsible for the actions of the governments in which or under which they serve is a recent one, and it is in conformity with the historical growth of law out of primitive custom, which shows a uniform movement away from collective and towards individual responsibility for lawless conduct. It seems probable that sooner or later international law, if it is to become effective, must take this path. The stumbling block is the central position of the sovereign state in international thought. There is a logical collision between the doctrine of sovereignty and the concept of the rule of law, however these be formulated, which is manifest in all attempts to fix the blame for unlawful behaviour upon men rather than upon nations. It has hitherto been taken for granted that, as a general rule, before any action can be taken against an individual for a breach of international Law the acquiescence of the state of which he is a citizen must be obtained, either by formal agreement or voluntary acceptance of the jurisdiction of a tribunal, or by forced submission to a victorious power [1]. The German and Japanese War Crimes Trials were not a departure from, but an illustration of this basic assumption.

It is not proposed here to examine the pros and cons of the War Crimes Trials, but only to distinguish those proceedings from the suggestion presently to be advanced for the judgment and restraint of individuals who in all the manifold relationships of international life today may from time to time offend against the rules or principles of international law binding upon the countries in whose name they issue orders.

In the existing system of international law it is axiomatic that no new legal rule can be imposed upon a sovereign state without its consent. It is likewise axiomatic that a state cannot be judged by an international tribunal unless it consents to the jurisdiction either by a preliminary general acceptance of an international convention instituting the court, or by *ad hoc* submission in a particular case. It has hitherto been thought that from these two axioms it must follow that individual servants of a particular state cannot be brought to judgement for an allegedly illegal action of that state unless it be a party to such a convention, or unless it acquiesces. In national law which regulates the relations between private citizens consent induced by duress invalidates an agreement. This principle has never made any great headway in international law. Agreements of various descriptions, and in particular peace treaties, are no wit less valid in international law by reason of the fact that they are sometimes extracted by economic pressure, military threats or actual conquest unless it can be proved that the treaty was imposed by an aggressor [2]. Negotiation there may be, but it is sometimes of an order which, in private litigation, would disentitle a plaintiff to redress for breach of contract. A state on the brink of defeat in war will sue for peace, and the resulting agreement gives rise to consequences which are deemed to be, and in the existing system certainly are, legally unchallengeable. It is not, for instance, possible to conceive of Germany, Italy, or Japan putting forward any legal claim to territory detached from their rule by the various treaties and arrangements establishing their frontiers after the first and second world wars. In international life the plea of *force majeure* makes no legal impact at all, and practically no political impact, unless and until that plea is backed by the threat or use of force.

The law creating role of force in international life being thus admitted, and the policy of unconditional surrender having been pursued to the bitter end in 1945, it was easy for the victors to claim the right, for which there were numerous precedents,[3] to judge and punish enemy offenders against the laws of war. The idea of making individuals responsible for the illegal conduct of the states they serve was an undoubted advance, but the attempts since made under the direction of the General Assembly of the United Nations,[4] to establish this idea permanently in international life have proved abortive because the notion of consent includes, in international law as it is today, the notion of forced submission. A nation might very well consent to a convention giving an international tribunal jurisdiction over its statesmen and servants, but it will not consent, *in limine*, to the use of external force to secure the persons of the accused. Even if it were to agree to use its own internal police force to arrest and deliver an accused Minister into the custody of an international tribunal, it will not consent to be forced to do so. It would not permit its own police to be policed.

The adoption and enforcement of an international criminal code applicable to politicians is thus not practicable. The contradiction between the doctrine of sovereignty and the rule of law previously referred to is a radical fault in the existing system of international law. This has been widely recognized by those who advocate a World Security Authority, an international Police Force, Federal Union, World Government and many draft proposals for Charter revision. All these suggestions imply and sometimes express the view that the concurring nations should yield some part of their sovereignty to a central authority. Sovereignty can only be yielded by consent or snatched by force from a defeated government, and the consent or forced submission must be a continuing consent or submission. However unreservedly a state might frame its accession to a legal instrument establishing a central authority either executive or judicial, the leading statesmen responsible for its international conduct could not be compelled to submit without the threat or use of force, for they would never themselves voluntarily consent to the execution of a command issued by international authority if they deemed it to be contrary to the rights and interests of the state they governed, and for whose welfare they were responsible. A central authority would therefore always have to be armed with overwhelming force if it were to discharge, among other functions, that of disciplining the responsible political leaders of a recalcitrant state.

It is the purpose of this book to suggest and describe a mode of discipline which could be applied without the backing of a central military force, without cession of sovereignty, and without either the consent or forced submission of the state whose leading politicians and officials are judged guilty of internationally illegal conduct. Furthermore if this method of discipline were to be applied it will be shown that the stumbling block of national sovereignty which admittedly obstructs the development of international law, and prevents it from assuming a compulsory character, can be circumvented, So far from calling upon the nations to renounce their sovereign rights, which they would probably never do voluntarily, it points out a way, perhaps the only immediately feasible way, whereby they can safely retain these rights, and by making intelligent use of them, subject those who direct international policies to the control of law. Before describing the proposal it is, however, desirable to consider how the character of the international sovereign person of present day international law, that is to say the modern nation state, differs from the sovereign persons of the seventeenth century whom the early European writers had in mind when they first formulated the principles of behaviour known to us as International Law.

These early writers on International Law addressed European kings, not the Emperor of China, nor the Mogul rulers of India nor African tribesmen, nor the Americas. Recognising the fact of sovereignty, they appealed to the consciences of individual men, the rulers of the newly risen European States, who shared a common culture, a common language for the inter-change of thought and a common inheritance of legal principles and ethical standards. The focal point, the person bound, by the international obligations of Grotius' day was a human being exercising sovereign power, but personally responsive to the same principles as his brother sovereigns. The international situation today offers a parallel and a contrast. National sentiment is rising all through Africa, the Near East and Southern Asia, but on the other hand sovereignty has changed.

Absolute sovereignty has always been a political myth, for no state, not even imperial Rome, has ever been free to do exactly as it liked. Every king or emperor, however despotic at home, and however powerful abroad, has always had to consider the probable reactions of friendly or unfriendly neighbours to his foreign policy, and this necessity has increased with the growth of communications. The political, economic and military interdependence of states now seems to have reached a point where the sovereignty of most states is becoming unreal. It remains as an idol in men's minds. Lawyers distinguish between sovereignty *de jure* and sovereignty *de facto*, the former being the right to exercise power, and the latter its actual exercise. In another dimension of thought the conception of sovereignty may be divided into its internal and external aspects. With certain exceptions the nation states today have internal sovereignty, that is to say they enjoy the right and power of self government, without interference from other powers. The exceptions are the communist satellite states which possess internal *de jure* sovereignty, but they cannot freely exercise their right to determine their own form of government. It may be that the majority of their populations believe in communism in some form or other, but their *de facto* sovereignty is subject to that of Russia to the point that they cannot develop communist theory, let alone any other kind of political or economic theory, as they please.

The internal sovereignty of the vast majority of states remains intact. It is the external *de facto* sovereignty of almost all states which has diminished since the second world war. Not even Great Britain and France, which are still classed as great powers and possess the right of veto in the Security Council of the United Nations have the power to take independent action and carry it through to a predetermined conclusion, as was illustrated by the Suez crisis of November 1956. Interdependence is less a chosen policy than a description of facts. In varying degrees the *de facto* external sovereignty of nations is dissolving into an inchoate tangle of agreements, economic pressures, military necessities and moral ideas. Only Russia, Red China and the United States are strong enough to steer self-chosen courses, and they alone retain separate *de facto* sovereignty in world affairs. National sovereignty appears to be crumbling.

The existing system of international law was built round the concept of sovereignty. Its purpose was to control the relationships of supreme rulers, and it was not and is not designed to deal with the confused and uncontrollable relationships of governments which are subject to so many conflicting pressures that no one of them can maintain a consistent separate policy.

What is needed is a new concept of international law not entirely dependent for its growth upon the agreement of sovereigns, for a mere agreement cannot have contractual force unless it is contained within and enjoys the *imprimatur* of a superior and compulsory legal order. Every system of national law provides elaborate criteria for determining which agreements shall and which shall not be enforced by its courts. In most systems a defined degree of mutuality is required, that is to say both parties must freely perform or promise to perform some act for the benefit of the other. Otherwise the agreement is binding only in honour or unenforceable by reason of improper pressure.

2

Analysis of international sanction

Because the persons of early international law were sovereign monarchs there was no place in the writings of early international lawyers for Law enforcement by the decisions of international Courts, or for police action, and this perhaps accounts in part for the failure of attempts made to introduce sanctions into the League Covenant and the United Nations Charter. There is an inconsistency in the concept of sanctions as expressed in the doctrine of collective security, much in vogue between the world wars.

In all the debates since the first world war international lawyers seem to have lost sight of the whole meaning of legal sanction, which is the fear, before action is taken, that some unpleasant consequence will certainly follow an action in breach of the law. In truth the word sanction has two aspects. The primary one is antecedent fear of a penalty, the second is forcible prevention of an unlawful action and civil correction or penal action after the event. The sanctions provided for in the Covenant of the League of Nations, and in the Charter of the United Nations belong in the second class. They have never operated in the primary sense because their imposition has always been a matter of political calculation, not the certain consequence of a Court Order. The doctrine of collective security has never been put into operation successfully, except in the case of the Korean war, but in this case the American and Associated troops were only able lawfully to fight under the United Nations flag, because Russia, foolishly from her own point of view, withdrew her representative from the Security Council, which was thus able to make a decision without the impediment of the Russian veto.

Many consider the North Atlantic Treaty Organisation to be a successful experiment with the doctrine of collective security, but it is not so in the sense of either the Covenant or the Charter. Collective security was originally meant to be the common military action of the Member States against any one of their number which used or threatened violence against another, contrary to the agreements, to further its own political ends. The North Atlantic Treaty Organisation is not designed for this purpose. It is a defensive alliance of a number of States of variable power against the possible aggression or military threats of one group of the members of the United Nations, Russia and her satellites. It is easy to say that this Organisation could be used against any aggressor within the group of the NATO Powers, but those closely associated with the Organisation know well that this is legally and militarily impossible. It is legally impossible because the NATO Council can only make decisions if all members are agreed. The resulting legal difficulty became evident during a dispute between Turkey and Greece over the Cyprus issue. Both countries are members of NATO. Had the quarrel between them reached the point of violence, NATO could not lawfully have intervened to keep the peace without the consent of both. Even if a majority of the NATO Council had decided that one or the other was exclusively at fault, no legal intervention would have been possible within the NATO framework. NATO is not therefore a manifestation of the real doctrine of collective security, as it is not empowered to keep order among its own members, but only to act as an organ of collective defence against an outsider.

NATO is the consequence of the weakness of the Security Council system. It is true that if any one or more of the members of the United Nations were to use violence, the Security Council could take military action, but only if the powers possessing the right of yeto were in agreement. As Russia and the Western Powers are respectively addicted to taking opposite sides in any international conflict, military sanctions are problematical, and if there is any doubt in the mind of a would-be Law breaker as to whether or not action will be taken against him, the sanction loses its primary character which is to prevent unlawful behaviour by fear of the consequences rather than to restrain or correct it by force during or after the event.

The ineptitude of the collective security doctrine is even more apparent in the hypothetical case, which may well not remain hypothetical, of an outbreak of lawless violence between the veto powers. In such a case the United Nations would be legally disentitled and physically unable to keep order among its own members, just as is NATO.[5]

The military objections to the doctrine of collective security are even greater than the legal ones and more practically convincing. War today is a complex and widespread social operation. It involves whole populations and their industries, and therefore it must be planned beforehand, as it is being planned today by the United States and her Western allies and as it is also certainly being planned by Russia and her allies. Planning does not always imply the intention to execute the plan. It is possible and, one hopes, probable that Russia has no more intention of attacking Western Europe or North America than *vice versa*. But a defensive military plan must take into account primarily the principal source of danger, that is to say it must be aimed. This is not true of the military planning of any single government which prepares for operations in all conceivable conflicts, neither is it true in the case of a small scale international operation involving contingents from one or more national armies, but it is true in the case of total war, involving the whole of the United Nations, and military force on this unlimited scale would be required to control a major state. It would thus be impossible for a United Nations General Staff, or the General Staff of a World Federal Government, to plan the application of military sanctions against an unspecified member.

Recognition of this difficulty led to the establishment of NATO which is the political planning Staff of some of the principal Western members of the United Nations designed to restrain that member which is thought to be the most likely to commit a breach of the peace, but NATO is necessarily outside the framework of the United Nations Organisation, and not subject to the control or supervision of the Security Council or the General Assembly.

At the time of the establishment of NATO, no armed attack had occurred, but there was manifest danger, as there still is, of a Communist intrusion into Western Europe, whether by direct military advance or, as was and still is more likely, by planned political coups, followed by military support from Russia. The planners of NATO were merely being realistic in recognising that a political and military invasion of non-Communist areas by the Communists could not be withstood unless a combined plan of defence were made at once. They realised that defensive war needs to be planned just as much as offensive war, but that the United Nations cannot by reason of its almost universal character plan defensive war against any one of its own members and in particular not against one of the veto powers. NATO is however, an organisation outside the United Nations security scheme, and has no relations with the Security Council. From the point of view of those who desire to establish orderly relations between states under the rule of Law, it would be better to recognise the fact and in recognizing it to acknowledge that International Law as we know it, founded upon the principle of good faith between rulers cannot find a place for the universal enforcement of its obligations by physical force short of war. That is not to say that there is no use for force in international affairs. It has been said that the function of force is to give moral ideas time to take root. Possibly this is the service that NATO may render to the world. Even nuclear armaments may serve this end, but it should be understood that no combination of forces, no specific armaments, and no defence planning, can secure the rule of law for the world.

Peace is not the proper goal of international politics.[6] Peace is a by-product of orderly civic life, just as happiness is a by-product of an orderly private life. If peace or happiness are pursued, the means of pursuit will destroy the goal.

> "He who bends to himself a joy
> Doth the wingèd life destroy." [7]

This exposes the fallacy of the old argument *si vis pacem para bellum.* Desire for peace leads men to prepare for war, and always in the end we have had war and not peace, destroying what we sought to hold. It is a common opinion that World War II broke out because Britain and France were insufficiently prepared for war, and that had they been able to attack or convincingly threaten Germany on the occasion of one of Hitler's earlier *coups*, war could have been avoided. No one however allows for the fact that a nation which has peace as its primary goal cannot seriously threaten war until it feels compelled by imminent danger, thus giving an aggressive state the initial advantage and so ensuring war. Peace will result from law and order, but law and order will never grow out of the armed truces which are all the twentieth century knows of peace.

The moral ideas which must emerge while NATO and the nuclear missiles maintain the truce have been formulated in the principles of the United Nations Charter, and in the Universal Declaration of Human Rights. No sanction is, however, applicable to breaches of these principles because even those who hold that war is the ultimate sanction of international law, would not maintain that war or the threat of war either could or ought to be used in every case to uphold the principles of the Charter or the Declaration of Human Rights when these are infringed.

The problem before the world now is how to make international law into effective law. It is debatable whether law is the cause or the effect of ordered human life, but both the *Pax Romana* and the *Pax Britannica*, throughout the centuries when they prevailed, were based on law, and it seems evident that a *Pax Mundi* must also be based on law. Whether it is at present possible to create a world law is very doubtful. The common mind of peoples is perhaps so undisciplined that it cannot evolve a legal system on an international scale. This is however not certainly the case, and to believe it leads to despair. It is better, "to hope till hope creates from its own wreck the thing it contemplates."[8] Would not the best way to set about translating hope into achievement be, instead of attempting to transform the world by blueprints, to educate and gradually control the men who play a part in international affairs? The weakness of traditional international law, which purported to know only states, and ignored individuals is that its rules, often antiquated and uncertain, find little echo in the consciences of individuals, so that the whole feeling of responsibility of statesmen, officials and diplomats is turned exclusively towards their own government and people, and takes very little account of the disapproval of the rest of the world.

The proposal now to be made for strengthening international law is to make individuals responsible for its application, but only in so far as it is practicable to impose some penalty upon a law breaker without seizing his person or property. Arrest and seizure would not be feasible except by using physical force against the state in whose name an unlawful act had been committed, and within whose territory the culprit can take refuge with his goods and chattels intact. Civilisation is a long way from international warrants of arrest or writs of attachment, but if mankind could abandon its tendency to anarchy, a machinery of law enforcement with the minimum use of actual force might be devised. If it is not, the only enduring peace which seems likely is the peace of death.

International law is at present concerned primarily with states and their relationships, seldom directly with human beings, nor even with the big international companies. It is not, even now, entirely true to say that the only "persons" in international law are states, and that these alone have rights and duties according to international law. The European convention on Human Rights and the Red Cross Conventions of 1949 bestow certain rights and duties under international law directly upon individuals. Moreover although individuals may not be parties before the Court of International Justice at the Hague,[9] there are precedents for private litigants before other international courts, such as the *Tribunaux Arbitraux Mixtes* after the first World war.

In practice however, it is usually states or interstate agencies which are entitled to rights and subject to duties under the rules of international law. Scores of proposals have been made before and since Nuremberg for some form of international criminal jurisdiction dealing with terrorism, war crimes, breaches of the Hague Conventions of 1907 on the laws of war, crimes against the peace, crimes against humanity and genocide. The idea of a permanent Court operating in peacetime, as well as at the end of a war, has failed time and again, and the reason seems to be that the proposals for such an institution have not fitted existing conditions. Crime is an offence which concerns the whole of society to which a man owes his duty, not merely the particular person who has been robbed or attacked. It is a rejection of the duty of obedience a man owes to his country. There is no international focus of duty at present, and everyone owes political, legal and personal allegiance to the state of which he is a citizen. The notion of international crime therefore hardly makes sense, for crime involves an anti-social action endangering the whole community whose interests all citizens are in duty bound to respect. The actions which have been suggested as proper subjects for international criminal judgment are, in this context, unsuitable, for they have been performed for the benefit of the state to which the accused men owe their allegiance. The acts and intentions are political and should be judged with reference to the appropriate focus of loyalty. They are admittedly odious and cruel by humanitarian standards, but it is nevertheless unfair to ignore their political context, which is relevant in assessing moral responsibility. an essential feature of crime. There can be no acceptable criminal law not based upon a common code of duty. Breaches of international law of whatsoever degree should not therefore be treated as common crimes. Individuals must be made subject to international law and held answerable for breaches of it, but not regarded as criminals in the same sense as the prison population of a nation state. All criminal law acknowledges degrees of crime, and Anglo-Saxon readers will be familiar at least with the words "felony" and "misdemeanour" and will know that there are many minor offences which carry little blame. The Common Law of England however does not provide a pattern which would be readily adaptable to international law. Continental law offers more promising analogies for meeting the present international situation.

3

International delinquency

No widely accepted classification of punishable wrong-doing, capable of adaptation to international affairs, has ever been evolved, either by English or by Latin legal talent. Modern Continental codes however illuminate the moral element of law better than the common law tradition. The codes divide crimes into three classes, and German codes and commentaries provide the best illustration. According to the code of 1871, crimes are either major crimes (*Verbrechen*), minor crimes (*Vergehen*), or petty offences (*Übertretung*). The corresponding French terms are *crime*, *délit* and *contravention*. According to one German commentator, Kohlrausch,[10] the tripartite division of offences was derived from philosophical doctrines of the early nineteenth century. A wrong was conceived as criminal in different degrees according to the nature of the right violated. Wrongs against natural inherent rights (*angeborene Rechte*) were considered as major crimes, (German *Verbrechen*; French *crime*). Wrongs against rights acquired by virtue of membership in an organized body politic were minor crimes (German *Vergehen*; French *délit*). An act of disobedience to an order was a petty offence (German *Übertretung*; French *contravention*).

The philosophical basis of this threefold classification has never been followed in practice and is not universally accepted. The verbal classification is used, but the words are related to the type of punishment inflicted and not to the nature of the right violated or the status of the rule infringed. Thus murder is classed as a crime in all continental codes, not because it is a wrong against the natural inherent right to live, but because it has been made statutorily punishable by death, or long imprisonment in a penitentiary. The severity of the punishment has been legislatively fixed to match the gravity of the crime, and is thus indirectly related to the right violated, so that the three philosophical classes have had due effect in framing the penal laws, but the verbal definitions found in the codes ignore the ethical grounds on which, according to some commentators, the classification is based. Thus, in the introductory provisions of the German code of 1871, "a major crime is any act punishable by death or by confinement in a penitentiary, or by confinement in excess of five years in a fortress." If the ethical basis had been used the definition should have been that a major crime is an unlawful act infringing the natural or inherent rights of man; but perhaps a definition of natural or inherent rights of man would tax too far the ingenuity of legal draftsmen.

For present international purposes the continental classification of wrong-doing is useful because the historical basis of it is a consciously thought-out classification of rights and duties. International law now deals mostly with the rights and duties of states, which are not natural entities in the same sense as man. There are numerous definitions of the word "state" varying between the simple declaration *l'état, c'est moi* of an absolute monarchy, to the communist claim that when true communism is universally established states will cease to exist. The different definitions do not, however, always describe the same thing, but frequently describe different social conditions at different times in history, whereas any definition of "a man" always relates to the same object. From the point of view of the law therefore, the natural and inherent rights of man (whatever they may be) are distinguishable in character from the rights of states. In devising future penal international law therefore it is logically possible to ignore the whole group of "natural and inherent rights," breaches of which constitute major crimes, and to concentrate on the second type of rights referred to by Kohlrausch as rights acquired from society. At present the world is a badly organized society, but the purpose of all sane policy must be to organize it better. International law-breaking should therefore be treated as the type of wrong-doing dealt with in continental codes under the heading of *Vergehen* or *délits*, which can be translated into English as delicts or delinquencies. Both because of the absence of any international focus of duty, and because the rights of states are in a different category from the natural and inherent rights of man, the world is not ripe for an international criminal code. It is true that international wrong-doing, if it involves physical violence, causes death and bodily injury to men, thus violating their natural rights, but from the standpoint of classical international law responsibility lies in the state not in its servants.

Although therefore there is at present no place for an international penal code providing for direct criminal responsibility across the boundaries of nation states, breaches of international law ought to be punished, where they are judged to be wrong, account being taken in assessing blame, of the patriotic duty a man owes to his own country.

A system of penal law not containing a moral element could not thrive. The arbitrary use of power is not lawful authority, so that even if some centralised organ of the international community were to become the sole repository of power, there would still not necessarily be any rule of law in the world, though there might be tyranny; and international tyranny is not an imaginary spectre to be dismissed by contemporary political realists. It has happened before now that a whole nation, sick of disorder and civil war, has submitted to a tyrant simply for the sake of quietude. This could very well happen over the whole earth and will, if further world wars break out. The only safeguard is law, not bombs. Slowly the peoples of the world must learn to withdraw their confidence from rulers who are wanton international law breakers. Wantonness is suggested as the key factor in international delinquency. The word here is intended to imply a reckless and unwarrantable defiance of international obligations. It implies guilt, but not the guilt of the common thief or assassin. Illustrations sufficient to guide a court in determining wantonness are to be found in all national legal systems. In English Law, for instance, blackmail is defined in part as a demand for money with menaces *without reasonable or probable cause.*[11] Again, part of the definition of fraud is to make an untrue statement *recklessly, not caring whether it be true or false.*[12] In determining *mens rea* – the guilty mind – when judging these crimes the court makes a subjective judgment much more individual and profound than in cases of theft, murder and other felonies where, for the most part, the act alone demonstrates the guilty intent unless the accused can adduce special explanatory factors. The guilt of Hitler and his colleagues would be included but the conduct of men who, acting under political and economic pressure and being charged with responsibility for the safety and well-being of the people whom they rule, dishonour an international treaty obligation would sometimes be excluded. Thus true national loyalty would not be condemned, and conscientious men could hold high positions in the state without fear.

This is not to say that a plea of patriotic duty should always excuse a man for breaking the law, but it should be taken into account before he is declared to be an international delinquent, and in recommending a penalty. For instance, in 1956 the standing threat to Israel by all her Arab neighbours, the constant border raids, and the military alliance between Egypt and the other Arab countries threatened the very existence of Israel, so that the attack on the Sinai peninsula could be supported as a defensive act, and for that reason might be defended in law under article 51 of the Charter. The question for examination now is therefore what can be done to men who give orders contrary to International Law. Apart from the straightforward issue of legality, any judgment of guilt must take patriotism into account. No court machinery has ever been devised which can fully explore motive, and the moral judgments of men differ according to the political context of the action. A spy is a villain in an enemy country, but a hero in his own. For the sake of their countries men will perform acts which in every other context they would themselves condemn, and which are condemned by the citizens of all politically detached or unfriendly states. They will lie, cheat, imprison, kill and destroy, honestly believing themselves to be justified. Heads of states and their responsible ministers initiate policies which necessarily lead to all or some of these actions, but they are obeyed and kept in power because the people believe that these men are best able to serve the public well-being in their own countries.

4

The new sanction described

Classic International Law provides that certain actions may be taken by states against states if the rules are broken and damage suffered. Apart from certain special cases such as the German and Japanese War Crimes trials, and the United Nations Resolution of the 12th December 1946 in the General Assembly affirming the principles of the Nuremberg Charter there has never been any general provision for dealing with men who give internationally illegal orders, especially in time of peace.

One of the things that a state can do if it is offended by another state is to sever diplomatic relations. This is not a very forceful action, though it sometimes leads to a settlement by agreement. It is at present a political action taken only by states parties to a dispute, regardless of the legality or otherwise of the actions of the offending state, and it is taken only against a state. A subsidiary practice, which is related to this right to sever diplomatic relations, is the diplomatic practice, according to which a government may, and often does, take action against an individual diplomat from a foreign country by declaring him to be *persona non grata*. This action is taken if the government considers the behaviour of the diplomat to be offensive. Sometimes the conduct of which the offender is accused is spying, or other improper political activity, and sometimes it is mere lack of social decorum; but whatever the cause the diplomat has to be recalled. This is but a minor punishment, but it is directed against a person for his personal behaviour, and imposed by political authority. It is never the result of judicial decision.

The repudiation of one man on political grounds, by one government, for instance the refusal of the Netherlands to accept Mr. Molotov as Ambassador, could be adapted and developed for use internationally by giving to Courts of International Delinquency power to recommend that a politician, diplomat or other representative of one country who has officially given orders in breach of international obligations, should be treated as *persona non grata* by all states. Thus a man who was judged personally guilty of international delinquency could be repudiated by the whole community of nations. He would be denied recognition in the office which he held. Such a man could not travel outside his own country even on holiday. He could not conduct international negotiations, nor represent his government. His signature would be dishonoured on every international document subsequently issued under his authority, including the passports of his fellow countrymen and the credentials of delegates whom he thereafter purported to appoint. He would, in law and in fact, become incapable of acting in the international world. He would not be physically injured or imprisoned, even outside his own country; he would merely be sent home.

Outlawry is a universal sanction of primitive law. What gave it its power in the ancient world was an attendant superstitious horror. The outlaw was in a sense unclean and was deprived of social protection by his tribe. So far as we can now surmise it was the fear of being outcast, just as much as the fear of death, or hunger, or cold, which operated as a social sanction then, but whatever it may have been, it was psychological rather than physical force which constrained primitive man to conformity.

It is not possible to resurrect from the ancient world the fear of being cut off from the tribe, the fear of gods and demons, of death and the loss of social protection which constituted the sanction of primitive law, but it might be possible to restrain sophisticated politicians by striking at their weakest point, which is a combination of vanity and ambition. The collective rejection of a man by the international community might oust him for ever from the world stage where, if only in phantasy, such a man desires to play an heroic role. Exclusion from the international community would hurt his self-esteem and might eventually injure his career, which is what he cares about most, and it would cost nothing in either blood or money, except fees of Court and Counsel. Fear of pain and loss is the real sanction of Law, and this fear can be induced by other means than physical force.

Those who, reading this proposal for the first time, consider that the suggested sanction is too weak to have any compelling power, should reflect that banishment from the company of one's fellows is the fundamental social sanction in all communities. Exclusion from clubs or from professional organisations operates effectively to secure certain standards of conduct by those who belong, and pride themselves in belonging to the choicest social groups or professions. Moreover, though we are accustomed today to think that the proper fate of a law breaker is imprisonment this penalty is in essence exclusion from society. The primitive world had no prisons – only outlawry or banishment were practicable. Even the death penalty itself, though other elements enter in, is the final sentence of exclusion imposed by men upon a dangerous member of the human race.

It is admitted that even if the sanction were to be applied to a Foreign minister judged delinquent, and had the effect of making him incapable of carrying out his functions so that he had to be replaced by another, there would be nothing to prevent a determined government from appointing another foreign minister who would carry on the same policy. In this case the sanction would have failed in its primary purpose which is to restrain law-breaking before it occurs, just as national criminal law fails every time an offence is committed. It is the initial function of sanction which is lacking in international law today, and which the suggestion made in this book is designed to supply. The prospect that one's policy will be carried on by another would be no consolation to an ambitious politician so that the strength of the primary sanction would not be weakened by its inefficacity as a secondary or corrective sanction.

Lawbreaking politicians could not be arrested personally without making war on the state in whose name they had acted. From the point of view of legal procedure the objection to using force to bring an accused man before a Court is that the war would first have to be fought and won, and in the course of such a conflict the original issues might be lost to sight. The practical and political objections to the use of war as a legal instrument are obvious. It is not possible to go to war at a moment's notice, since a warlike mood must develop in people's minds. Today war does not involve merely armed forces. Whole peoples with their industrial and agricultural resources are engaged. Collective wrath, fear and hate are prerequisites. Even if an accused politician belonged to a relatively small and weak state the use of force against him would be impracticable, for no state today exists in a political vacuum. When international tension occurs, the focal point of trouble may be in the early stages only a quarrel between two states, but surrounding nations, and other nations all over the earth, with world-wide interests or political sympathies one side or the other, become involved. A catscradle of conflicting interests, political pressure and misrepresentation ensues, and results in dangerous and unmanageable confusion. Moreover there is a disproportion between the discipline suited to an individual delinquent and the havoc of war.

Since only war is a sufficient force to secure compliance with the summons of an International Court, and since it is an impracticable and inefficient instrument, it is necessary to devise legal procedure not requiring the physical presence of the defendant, yet not allowing judgment to go by default in his absence. It is essential that the case of an accused politician, which would of course be the same as that of the state in whose name he had acted, should be fully argued before judges. In law there would be no difficulty about this, as the court could appoint an independent lawyer to represent the defendant and meet the argument of the accuser. The difficulty would be to get at the facts if the defendant and his government boycotted the proceedings. Most countries would probably cooperate to some extent, and would not allow a public argument to go on in an international court, based on the accuser's version of the facts. By some means or other they would state their own case, if only for domestic consumption. At the same time they would no doubt repudiate a jurisdiction exercised without their consent. It is nevertheless vital that the jurisdiction should be so exercised, for if the jurisdiction is established by treaty, or any other technical variation of international agreement, it would always be possible for signatory states to make reservations or withdraw from the agreement, as witness the reservations made by the United Kingdom and nearly all other countries to the "compulsory jurisdiction" clause of the statute of the International Court of Justice.

As has been truly said the jurisdiction of that court is not compulsory.[13] Article 36 of the Statute provides that the court shall have jurisdiction over all cases referred to it and all matters specially provided for in the Charter or in treaties or conventions in force. All this jurisdiction is thus purely voluntary for it depends upon the agreement of states. The same article goes on to say in paragraph 2 that states may recognize the compulsory jurisdiction of the court over certain classes of cases, but in paragraph 3 it is said that this recognition may be made on condition of reciprocity on the part of several or of particular states, or that it may be only for a time. Among other states the United Kingdom has accepted the compulsory jurisdiction of the court, but this acceptance is now subject to nine reservations among which are "disputes arising out of, or having reference to, any hostilities, war, state of war, or belligerent occupation in which the Government of the United Kingdom are or have been involved." The acceptance is moreover only made until such time as notice is given to terminate it. This is not an acceptance of compulsory jurisdiction at all; it is jurisdiction by consent. While the states were sovereign in fact and in law, no other kind of jurisdiction would have been possible. Now, however, that only two of all the members of the United Nations retain anything approaching full *de facto* sovereignty, the time has come to act as a community in the primitive sense and set up courts to judge breaches of the law. There is no need for the peoples of the world to take any further action to form themselves into a community, they are a community in fact. Law is rooted in facts. Out of the facts of family life, the actual relationships of husband, wife, parents and children, the laws governing the family evolved; commercial law arose out of the dealings of merchants. It is not possible to make world order by making an arbitrary plan and drafting a set of rules. Apart from the fact that no government today would consider a proposal for a World Constitution, it would not, if adopted, be a forward movement. Those who advocate "World Government" as a formula do disservice to the cause they have at heart, which is world order. A written constitution for the world making provision for courts, for parliament and for offices of state comparable to cabinet offices in national government, would itself be based on consent, and would be binding only upon those states which consented, not upon the others, and only upon consenting states for so long as political circumstances in which they gave their consent remained substantially unchanged. International law as we know it today leaves too many ways open for the repudiation of treaty obligations for a constitutional document based upon consent to become effective law.

The community of nations can, even today, judge its

members by passing resolutions, but an assembly of hundreds is not a suitable machine for ascertaining the law, nor for assessing the guilt or innocence of individual politicians. The General Assembly of the United Nations is not a judicial assembly, but it is historically analogous to the tribal assemblies, the early councils, the meetings of the heads of families and of chieftains, which in primitive communities carried out the functions of government including judging and banishing from the society of their fellows those who would not obey.

The next question to be considered is whether or not the United Nations has authority to set up a court of international delinquency by resolution. The preamble, the statement of purposes and principles, and indeed the whole Charter is a legal haze. Professor Kelsen has done a superhuman task in his work on the Law of the United Nations. This great commentary has come near to giving to the Charter one of the qualities of law, namely the capacity for explicit interpretation. Nevertheless, the relevant phrases in the preamble and in the first article are so general that one could conclude that nearly anything could be done by the United Nations which would "establish conditions under which justice and respect for the obligations arising from treaties and other sources of international law can be maintained." It is in the articles of the Charter which set out the functions of the different organs that a rather more precise idea of what the organisation is lawfully entitled to do should be sought. The conclusions to be drawn are however negative. It is possible to say with some certainty what each organ may not do, but difficult to be precise about what it can do.

Articles 10 to 17 inclusive, which set out the functions of the General Assembly, contain the following main verbs: "the General Assembly may discuss – may consider – may call the attention of the Security Council – shall initiate studies – may recommend measures – shall receive and consider reports – shall consider and approve the budget ..." The impression given is that the Assembly can sit and think and talk but can never act.

Article 22 however provides that it can 'establish such subsidiary organs as it deems necessary for the performance of its functions.' Again however one has to be able to define a function of the Assembly before being sure that a subsidiary organ can be created to perform it. This power has been used to a considerable extent, in order to establish quasi-military organizations to keep the peace on the borders of Israel and to control disorder and fill the administrative gap in the Congo. The United Nations has established relief organisations in Korea and in the Middle East which do a great deal of practical work. It has set up one administrative tribunal on the lines of the International Labour Office tribunal, to deal with the claims of staff members aggrieved by their treatment at the hands of the Secretary General. This tribunal, though not composed necessarily of professional judges, is a true Court in that its judgments are binding upon the whole United Nations organisation, and establish the rights and obligations of the parties within its jurisdiction. There is no reason why the Assembly, which can pass resolutions concerning the conduct of states and by reason of Article 14 'recommending measures for the peaceful adjustment of any situation,' should not set up a judicial organ to try the legality or otherwise of international conduct and to judge the degree of blame to be attached to the actions of responsible ministers and other public servants.

The scope of such a judicial authority could be determined in the resolution, and funds provided by an appropriation. Such a move would provoke some opposition, and, having regard to the fact that it would be a new departure in the history of the United Nations, it should be passed by a two thirds majority vote under Article 18. If the Security Council were to sponsor such a plan there would be no ground to challenge its legality, for the Security Council has power to act as well as to talk. For instance, Article 41 provides that the

Security Council may decide what measures, not involving the use of armed forces, are to be employed to give effect to its decisions, and may call upon the members of the United Nations to apply such measures. These 'may include ... the severance of diplomatic relations ...' There is nothing here to exclude a declaration that a delinquent politician is to be disqualified from international functions, and treated as *persona non grata*.

If it must be assumed that some members of the Security Council would veto any such proposal, the General Assembly could nevertheless establish a judicial organ to advise it or its members on matters of internationally delinquent behaviour. It is here submitted that it has legal authority to do this by the combined effect of Article 1, paragraphs 1 and 4, and Articles 10, 14 and 22. Put together, the relevant phrases of these articles give the General Assembly power to establish subsidiary organs for performing its functions, and one of these functions is to discuss any question within the scope of the Charter and make recommendations to the members of the United Nations so as to bring about by peaceful means and in conformity with the principles of justice and International Law, adjustment of disputes or situations which might lead to a breach of the peace. Any breach of International Law and especially any wanton breach or any unlawful intervention could obviously lead to a breach of the peace, and as the Assembly itself is not, by reason of its numbers, and its political complexion, a fit body to decide whether an action is lawful or not, it could reasonably set up an organ to adjudicate on the law, and assess the guilt of those responsible.

It is necessary to emphasize here that though a two thirds vote of the Assembly is not binding on the members in any legislative sense, since a resolution is not a treaty engagement and could not commit the dissenting members, yet the effect of such a vote when executed by the establishment of the court of delinquency would be to extend the sanction even to dissenting members, as the sanction could be applied to their ministers and officers of state however strenuously such states might oppose the policy. Thus the Foreign Minister of a dissenting state, if he were judged guilty of breaking any substantive rule of international law binding on his country, such as a breach of treaty to which his country was party, or breach of a general rule of customary law, could be treated as *persona non grata* by all the states favouring the use of the sanction in pursuance of a judicial recommendation. Every country enjoys, as a part of its sovereign status, the right and the power to refuse admission to any foreigner, and to refuse recognition to any representative of a foreign state, and to refuse recognition to foreign governments, and thus to their members, especially to foreign ministers whose every communication can be refused as of right. It follows that the rule of international law that no state can be bound by the decisions of others without its consent, can by the method suggested be circumvented in so far as enforcement procedure is concerned. No attempt should be made to impose new substantive rules of law, but the ministers and officers of all states, whether such states consent to or dissent from the machinery outlined in this book, can, without infraction of any existing rule or doctrine, be subject to international judgement and be made to suffer the penalty consequent upon an adverse finding of the judicial organ established by majority vote of the United Nations.

This debate would be the first test of international solidarity. Community sense may still be too weak, and political sympathy with the group of nations to which one belongs may still be too strong, to allow the adoption of the policy of the universal application of a recommendation of international outlawry. If the judicial machinery were established, however, either within or outside the framework of the United Nations, even partial disqualification of a wrong-doer would not be wholly insignificant.

5

The court of international delinquency

There are difficulties in the way of setting up Courts of International Delinquency. One of them is to find competent and impartial Judges. Intellect is needed, but this is not hard to find. Experience of the legal thought of other countries than one's own is essential, for otherwise the reasoning behind a judgment or its manner of expression might seem utterly unconvincing to both lawyers and people in a country vitally affected. Nine times out of ten a set of facts judged in one country will produce the same judgment as in another country under a different legal code, but this is not always so and especially not where the interests which conflict are international.

The people of continental Europe would not be satisfied by a judgment rendered by an Anglo-Saxon judge, and *vice-versa*. The Arabs would not be satisfied by the judgment of a Pakestani Moslem Judge, because they think that their concepts of law have been contaminated by the British influence in India. The people on either side of the iron curtain could not accept the judgment of one another's Judges. This is no doubt an underlying reason why all through the short history of the Court of International Justice there has been a demand for national representation. People of one culture do not trust the opinions of people of other cultures. Article 31 of the Statute of the Court therefore provides that if the Court includes on the Bench no Judge of the nationality of any party, that party may choose a Judge to sit with the others.

The integrity of foreign Judges is not suspect, but people do not believe that foreigners will be able to see their point of view, or understand their conception of justice. People who have never travelled extensively abroad do not realise that there can be more than one standard of behaviour. Hence, unhappily, comes that terrible contempt felt by the people of one nation for others which, excited by politicians and newspapers, is the worst of all the obstacles in the way of those who desire to see the world ruled by law. When therefore a Minister of State is to be judged, it is important that the Court should be so constituted as to carry conviction to the minds of the people of that state. This was probably the dominating factor in the minds of those who at the end of the first world war decided that those Germans who were politically and militarily responsible for the inception and conduct of that war should be judged by Germans under those provisions of International Law which had been, throughout the period of hostilities, part of the laws of Germany. As everyone knows the attempt was abortive. German courts would not condemn men whom they regarded as German patriots. This failure brought about the equal but opposite legal weakness of the Nuremburg trials after the second world war. Here the Germans were judged, not by themselves, but by their victorious enemies. In the first case justice was not done and in the second case it was not 'seen to be done' by reason of the absence of neutral judges. A large section of public opinion on the side of the conquerors of the Second World War defend the justice of Nuremberg, but even liberal-minded Germans, Italians and Japanese are unconvinced by the composition of the Court. International courts of law must be universally convincing if the law is to prevail.

In private civil litigation, or national criminal courts, the loser is inclined to sulk, but he does not reject or even challenge the authority of the court which rejects his argument. A convicted criminal accepts his fate more philosophically than the loser in civil litigation, confining his complaints to the social, political or domestic situation which he says compelled him to commit the crime. It is essential that some such acceptance of international jurisdiction should be brought about if the conviction of Ministers of State is to have the desired effect. This can only be done if the Court is so constructed as to command respect for its impartiality, and confidence in its understanding of the problem, from the points of view of the nations concerned. Such a Court would take a long time to mature. In order to command some confidence at the outset, it should be composed of professional Judges who are among the highest in the judicature in their own countries. Although legal knowledge is important and although the leading Judges of the member nations of the United Nations have a less extensive knowledge of international law than the academic lawyers who have made of that subject a life-long study, a judicial habit of mind is the most important factor. There is no substitute for the day-to-day practice of weighing evidence, disentangling allegations of fact from points of law and determining between counter arguments. Moreover it is busy men who do the best practical work. If an international case were just one case occupying a few days' work behind the scenes and a few days' work in court, it would be only a passing incident, albeit an important one, in the minds of the Judges who decided it, and not an 'occasion' as is every case brought before the Hague Court of International Justice or the Administrative Tribunals of New York and Geneva. Men seldom do their best work when they feel themselves to be on show. The consciousness that one is occupying a position of somewhat glamorous importance in the world stultifies the intellect, and all work is done best if it is just part of the day's work.

A panel of International Judges should therefore be appointed from among men who hold high judicial office in their own countries. The panel might well be large, possibly including principal Judges of all nations, but there should be a maximum and minimum number allowed to sit together to hear any one case.

What is the optimum number is a matter for debate. The fewer the better, since the law of diminishing returns applies to bodies of men called together to reach a decision. An odd number is essential as a majority decision must prevail. The decision of one Judge alone would not satisfy the people of contending states, and this therefore rules out the numbers one and three for a court of three judges often leaves one to make the decisions. There are objections to the number five as there must be both a president and a vice-president who would between them share the administrative business of organising the hearings, and they might come to form a 'corner' in International Law, so that if there were five Judges the two constant Judges would only have to convince one other in order to secure a majority. Seven is thus the minimum. The maximum should be as small as can be endured by politicians. A clean break should be made with the doctrine of representation of interested parties on the Court. Every other argument apart, there will never be any true International Law while this element is present. The essence of the judicial function is impartiality. In all civilized countries, if a Judge knows the parties, or if he has any personal interest in the case, he disqualifies himself voluntarily from adjudicating. Representation of a system of law is however possible even if national representation is excluded.

In order to maintain uniformity of case law, machinery for judicial review of questions of law by the existing Court of International Justice should be provided. This could be done without international agreement, and without modifying the statute of the Court. The General Assembly of the United Nations has power under Article 96 of the Charter to request the International Court of Justice to give an advisory opinion on any legal question. Paragraph 2 of that article provides that 'other organs of the United Nations ... authorised by the General Assembly may request advisory opinions on legal questions arising within the scope of their activities'. It would be undesirable for the Assembly by a political vote to request an advisory opinion in every case. If the Assembly were unwilling to give the Court of Delinquency power to demand an advisory opinion from the Hague it could appoint a subsidiary organ under Article 22 for the purpose of carrying cases to The Hague. Here it would be best to follow the continental legal structure, adapting the organ known as the 'Parquet' to international purposes.[14]

After a French law student has passed his qualifying examinations, he has to decide immediately whether he will follow the career of a Judge or of an Advocate. There is no promotion from advocacy to the Bench, as in England and the United States. If he decides to be a Judge, three different types of occupation may come his way at different times in his career. He may be a civil servant in the Ministry of Justice, or he may be a Judge in civil and criminal cases, or he may fill a role the nearest equivalent to which is that of prosecuting Counsel in Anglo-Saxon countries. In this last role, he is a member of the 'Parquet,' but because he is a servant of the Ministry of Justice and has the same professional status as a Judge, his function is much wider than that of an English or American Attorney General, or a simple prosecutor briefed from time to time by the authorities. His basic duty on behalf of the State is to see that justice is done in the particular case, but when he attains a high standing he has to watch over the whole field of law. One special function is exercised at the very top of the hierarchy of the French Parquet. This is the task of referring not a whole case but a particular point to a supreme court called the Court of Cassation, in the interests of the law. It is this particular function of the 'Parquet' which should be adapted to international use. A subsidiary organ of the United Nations should be charged with the task of referring points of law to the Hague Court and the Nations whose Ministers were accused of delinquency should not, and under the present Statute would not, have that right.

An International Parquet could play a valuable role in demanding and conducting prosecutions against individual men for international delinquency, but the organ would have to be realistically constituted. It would be no use delegating these tasks to theoretical jurists, however eminent. The more responsible the men appointed, the more their decisions would be respected. Individual nations considering themselves aggrieved should, of course, have the right to complain and accuse any man they deem responsible, and it would not again be politically possible to insist that the international Parquet should have power to negative an accusation. It ought, however, to supervise the case whether or not the accused minister or his National government intervened, so as to ensure properly conducted contentious proceedings. The constitution of the Parquet must be left for the consideration of lawyers trained in the latin tradition. This book, being in English, is addressed largely to those who have been reared in the Anglo-Saxon tradition, and to whom the conception of a Parquet is *terra incognita.*

6

The right to accuse

Every state must have the right to bring an accusation against a man for wanton illegality. There are however, other persons aggrieved by a breach of International Law who should be permitted access to a Court of Delinquency. For instance, the Anglo-Iranian Oil Company had cause to complain of the action of the Government of Iran in taking over the oil fields contrary to an Agreement, yet when the case came before the Hague Court, this held itself to have no jurisdiction. The Company could not appear and plead breach of the Agreement which had been set aside by Iran, and the United Kingdom, though interested, could not collect enough treaty law to give the Court jurisdiction to deal with the substance of the injury suffered.

International companies such as this and the Suez Canal Company, for example, ought to have access to an international Court. The Hague could not be given jurisdiction in such matters without a modification of the statute of the Court, and this would require the agreement of states.

An International Parquet should however have the deciding voice as to whether or not a case in which a company were to be the plaintiff or accuser, should be heard before an International Court. The Parquet should decide, not upon the merits of the dispute, but upon whether it would be in the interests of international justice for it to be judicially resolved. There ought to be some control over this litigation, because the directors of large financial concerns do not suffer from the squeamishness which besets diplomats. They are hard-boiled business men and have no timidity before the law, no false pride in their positions, and do not have to consider their promotion or political advancement. For them litigation is a natural recourse, whereas a major political decision taken after endless discussion throughout the echelons of government and involving all sorts of legally irrelevant factors is required before the foreign offices of the world resort to international tribunals.

In addition to the international companies there are other groups of people who should have the right of complaint in these courts. These are the people of the non-self-governing and trust territories who at present have no separate standing in International Law because they are not independent 'sovereign' states. They have no separate political voice in the General Assembly of the United Nations, and cannot be parties before The Hague Court. In spite of the very genuine efforts which were made by the draftsmen of the Charter to provide for their interests, these people are still dependent upon the goodwill of sympathetic states and individuals for either a political or a judicial hearing. This ought not to be so. From time to time these non-self-governing territories become centres of dangerous emotional tension, as for instance Algeria and Cyprus, whose political importance in world affairs far outstrips their economic or strategic value. The territory of South West Africa is practically a text book case on the colour issue. The populations of these territories have no constitutional machinery for producing a unified political voice and therefore they need the help of an international Parquet to present their case before the world. This would be a familiar task to those brought up in the latin legal tradition. It is simply part of the task of securing justice for all and making the law equal and coherent everywhere. Nevertheless, non-self-governing territories should not be allowed to embark upon frivolous litigation, and therefore their claims ought always to pass through an international Parquet; otherwise they would constantly sue the colonial ministers in order to attract the press, thus using a judicial process as propaganda.

Finally, there are the individuals who may be damaged by breaches of international law committed by national or international officials or political ministers. Because the wrong is small on the world stage, and provokes no danger of war, that is no reason why they should not have their rights judicially secured, nor should the 'important' men concerned be exempt from blame. If men do wrong, to whomsoever it may be done, they ought to be punished, and they could be punished, not by the crude forms of imprisonment, fines or death, but in the subtler way of disgracing them before the world by disqualifying them from action in the international community. This litigation should however be under control. Only after exhausting every other remedy should the individual be permitted by the Parquet to accuse a responsible minister or official of delinquency.

It is true that many, perhaps most of the cases which might be brought before a court of delinquency by these various accusers, might not arise out of sets of facts which could possibly cause war. It is however part of the thesis of this book that the mere avoidance of armed conflict is a negative and self-defeating political goal. It should not be so much abandoned as set on one side and replaced by the prior and positive goal of promoting international justice for all men and nations whether in groups or as individuals. The aim of the new sanction is primarily educative. Men who make decisions on international issues, however transient, and even politically petty, should be brought to a serious consideration of the law governing those issues. The risk of public disgrace will have this effect upon their minds, for everyone who has advised a political chief knows the extreme sensitiveness such men display in private to any possibility of loss of prestige. To show that a given course of action may result in any kind of censure is, in practice, a more compelling argument than mere legal reasoning which is at present often shrugged off as a technical triviality. Moreover the new sanction could not control events once a warlike mood had developed, and it was felt that circumstances presented a *casus belli*. Its aim is to prevent such a situation from ever arising by regulating the behaviour of politicians before their emotions and the public anger at a series of illegal actions have reached the point of danger.

The elements of international delinquency should be personal, deliberate and wanton breach of international law, causing damage to the plaintiff. Only an experienced lawyer can know just how many intricate problems are raised by every word of the preceding sentence. Therefore, in its initial stages an international legal claim or accusation should be subject to the scrutiny of experienced lawyers, not in order to decide the issues, but to make sure that they are lucidly formulated, to discriminate between legal and political arguments, and to ensure that both sides are arguing on the same issue.

7

The choice of a defendant

A more delicate task than the selection and approval of cases to be brought before an International Court of Delinquency is the choice of a defendant. This should not be the random choice of a plaintiff colony, company or individual, though a state should be free to choose a defendant, and the Foreign Secretary of every state would be the normal defendant by virtue of his office. The English doctrine of Cabinet responsibility is no bar to legal proceedings against a Minister of the Crown in the Courts of the United Kingdom, so that there is no objection of constitutional principle to a Foreign Minister being made party to international proceedings.

The constitutional operation of governments is so various, and the relations between a prime minister and a foreign minister and between all the members of a cabinet so dependent upon local custom, and upon the personalities who participate in the making of international decisions, that it is impossible to lay down any general rule as to the choice of a defendant in any particular class of cases; moreover the effect of the judgement and the sanction in each case would vary in each country. For these reasons the Parquet should exercise a large measure of control on the selection of the defendants. In the appendix a number of actual international incidents occuring during the post-war period are described and indications given as to the persons who would have been the proper defendants. The basic principle must be that whoever was really at fault must bear the blame whatever his position in the governmental hierarchy.

The responsibility of civil service advisers must however also be considered. Personal liability for violation of international law and the risk of international disqualification would in the first place cause a Foreign Minister to make serious investigations through his advisers as to the legality or otherwise of any proposed policy, and secondly compel his advisers, were they civil servants or political lawyers, to examine the law dispassionately and consider the situation with as little prejudice as if they were advising an important client about private business. It is just this which, at the present time, they will not or cannot do. If they are political lawyers, they are themselves involved in a policy in which a particular legal issue is but one, and perhaps in their eyes, only an unimportant factor, and if they are civil servants they are personally interested in pleasing the Minister whom they advise.

If a Foreign Minister were in danger of punishment, the wish to please would be supplanted by the desire to protect. Only lawyers who have played both roles, the part of the independent adviser to a private client and the part of a legal adviser in a government office, can know the difference.

In the one case the client comes as a suppliant asking aid, and to him the lawyer's word is law, but in the other the lawyer is summoned as a servant, and if his service is unpleasing he is not invited to further discussions. To the political chief his lawyer's opinion is a tool for use as policy dictates. Men of the initial intellectual calibre of senior governmental legal advisers could, at the bar of England, hope to earn £ 20,000 a year subject to the risk of failure, not for lack of brains, but for lack of luck or personality. In their present offices they can earn £ 4,000 a year and a knighthood and they have security and a pension. The discrepancy in income reflects the discrepancy in their value as lawyers. The legal advisors do not lack brains, but they lack the experience of responsibility for the life or death, the freedom or imprisonment, or the personal ruin of their clients. If they had this responsibility they would become the equals of their colleagues in the national courts.

The object of this book is to produce the rule of law itself, not the rule of lawyers. Law has not been produced by lawyers, but by the collective legal genius of certain nations; but if international life remains as it is, and international lawyers remain subservient to politicians, either because they are powerless theorists, or powerless civil servants, there can be no international legal order.

At present international law is thought to be of little account, as witness the statement in a leading article of the London Times on August 1st 1956, less than a week after Colonel Nasser had nationalised the Suez Canal, where it was said, 'Quibbling over whether or not he was 'legally entitled' to make the grab will delight the finicky and comfort the fainthearted, but entirely misses the real issues.' Those who are familiar with national law, whether as parties, counsel or judges, know that every detailed point of law is by reference to the human interest concerned, a legal quibble; yet it is by such 'quibbles' that the law is applied and made, and we live at peace with one another because we respect it as a whole, even if it is intricate, and at times falls short of justice.

The status and quality of present day international legal advisers are not of merely academic interest. They raise the question as to whether the advisers of Foreign Ministers should themselves be liable for delinquency on the ground that they may have conspired to defeat or evade the law. This problem concerns not only legal advisers, but all high-ranking civil servants. In most countries the power of the civil servant is considerable and this is no modern development. The fathers of Charlemagne were hereditary Mayors of the Palace of Frankish Kings and so the authors of an Empire which lasted a thousand years. English readers, acquainted only with the practice, in Great Britain almost a fetish, that the Minister alone is responsible for the action of his department, may be shocked at the idea of imposing personal responsibility upon the civil service adviser. Such is the force of this rule in Great Britain that a Minister will resign his office for a fault committed by men in his department, though he had no personal knowledge of it. This practice is the corollary of the constitutional victory of the House of Commons over all other organs of government. Humble in origin, the Commons waged a centuries long battle to secure dominance, and one part of their strategy was to exclude the King from their deliberations. It followed logically that the King's servants must be excluded from debates, and that therefore they are neither permitted, nor can be compelled, to answer politically for their actions to the people whose lives and liberties are gravely affected by their decisions. It does not however follow that these men should not be answerable to other nations. Where real power is, the men who hold it should be compelled to submit to judgment for what they do, and what they advise their political chiefs to do. It is true that there is no method of compelling the principal Foreign Office advisers to attend in person an International Court, any more than it is possible to compel a Foreign Minister to attend; but if held to blame they would be debarred from a wide field of foreign service, and in particular from holding the office of Ambassador which, for all its declining responsibility, is still the goal of the diplomat. Admittedly all nations may not immediately impose the penalty of international disqualification. The natural impulse of the remaining sovereign states, that is to say U.S.A., Russia and Red China, would be to repudiate the whole proposal for a sanction which would in the end subject them also to the rule of law, and thus strike at the roots of their sovereignty. Once the proposal were adopted by a two thirds majority of the United Nations, however, many states would apply the sanction. If a diplomat were known to be *persona non grata* either by reason of his own misbehaviour or that of the Minister who appointed him, he could scarcely hold the principal diplomatic posts in Washington, Moscow,

London or Paris. Such a man could not carry out his mission if he were disowned by two thirds of the Diplomatic Corps. This would be done on the instructions of governments acting in pursuance of a judicial recommendation against the man or the minister who appointed him – not against the state of which he was the pretended representative. Even the giant states, which might be tempted to defy an international judgment, could by this means be affected in the choice of their representatives.

To be affected by the law against one's consent is the first step leading towards the authority of law, for though government by consent is often taken as a definition of democracy, this consent is not the consent of individual lawbreakers, but the general consent of the community. Government by individual consent in each instance would be anarchy, and this is the state of the world. The middle way between tyranny and anarchy is the acknowledged supremacy of the law and to achieve this the people of very many countries may be willing to sacrifice the personal prestige of their statesmen, politicians, ambassadors and civil servants.

It would be very much more difficult in some countries than in others to apply this sanction to permanent officials, such as British civil servants who are constitutionally shielded by the Ministers of the Crown, and who if involved in some internationally illegal undertaking of the government of the day, could not oppose their political chiefs without risking their careers. In tyrannical states the subordinate would risk his life if he resisted his own government. This is not so in all countries however. For instance, the head of the American State Department and his staff can be made answerable to Congress, and there is nothing in the Constitution of the United States to prevent them from being answerable to an International Court. Their responsibility is personal, and so far as the senior appointments are concerned, the occupants are by no means always career civil servants. There is alternative work open to them should they choose to resign rather than participate in an illegal policy. In every country each case must be judged on its merits, and in judging the conduct of a senior government servant his personal situation and prospects could not, without injustice, be ignored.

This factor was taken into consideration in the trials of men accused of crimes against the peace, war crimes and crimes against humanity in Germany and the Far East, and also in analogous proceedings conducted by Allied Tribunals, after the Second World War. The Nuremberg Charter, in Article 8, provided that 'the fact that the defendant acted pursuant to the order of his government or of a superior shall not free him from responsibility, but may be considered in mitigation of punishment if the Tribunal determine that justice so requires.' The activities judged at Nuremberg and in the Allied Tribunals in Europe and the Far East were cruel attacks on human life rather than minor political illegalities; but the principle of mitigation remains valid. In the War Crimes Trials if a man had acted in pursuance of superior orders but subject to 'irresistible fear of immediate and extreme consequences' he was dealt with mercifully or even exonerated.

Wherever an internationally illegal action causes death or pain to innocent people it ought to be possible to inflict physical punishment, but the time has not yet come, and the international community has not yet power to impose a sufficient penalty upon the most violent international offenders. The only method of controlling such men is war, which as a sanction is legally unmanageable and would now be indiscriminately disastrous.

Initial international wrongdoing could however be controlled at an early stage before there is danger of bloodshed on a large scale, and so produce respect for International Law. Respect for law is not just a general idea of all men of goodwill that law ought to be obeyed, but a fear in the minds of those whose decisions are affected by it that if they disobey they will suffer. Minor breaches of law committed with impunity, or a succession of legally disputed incidents, can easily lead to a major breakdown of international order. Hence the value of imposing by court machinery the comparatively mild sanction of international disqualification upon men who will not otherwise be brought to take international law into serious consideration before making their decisions, for though they often, probably almost always, enquire what the relevant rules of international law are, they take only public opinion at home and abroad into account. A British civil servant representing his country once advised an international conference on a critical issue of legal principle in the following terms: 'I remember a professor many years ago in the University of Oxford telling us never to ask in a crisis "What are all the facts? What is the legal position? Never ask the question: What is the principle involved? Always ask: What is wise?" '[15] A more candid repudiation of law has probably never been made. Only immediate personal risk should exonerate a civil servant for participation in an illegal policy, just as under the Nuremberg Charter it was only the 'irresistible fear of immediate and extreme consequences' which was allowed as a plea in mitigation.

8

Heads of states

If Prime Ministers, Foreign Ministers and subordinate officials are to be internationally answerable for their decisions, there remains the inescapable problem of the liability of those heads of states who are the real holders of power. In some countries, such as the United States it is the head of the state who is ultimately responsible for all executive decisions. He is the chief executive and control of Congress over him is merely negative. Congress can refuse him funds, and it can decline his proposals where these require legislation, and the Senate can reject a treaty, but Congress has no power of positive command, so that the President is responsible for his decisions and should therefore logically be answerable internationally for all he does.

In many other states the situation is otherwise. The King or President is the titular head of the state, the real decisions being taken by the Prime Minister and his Cabinet. This is the case in Great Britain. Depending upon the personality of the monarch, great or less influence can be exercised by him or her upon public affairs; but the influence is remote, and no situation is now likely to arise in which the Queen of England, for example, could be judged personally guilty of a breach of international law, even though she may, on the advice of her Prime Minister, sign an illegal order. In such a case neither she, nor anyone in her position, could have a free choice, and therefore the Constitutions of each country must be examined to see where real power lies.

The states of the world have constitutional arrangements capable of classification into three main groups with reference to the seat of executive power. The first is the Eurasian which consists of a head of the state, either hereditary or elected, a Prime Minister, a council of Ministers and a parliament. Sometimes one or more of these organs is missing, and the distribution of real power among them varies from country to country. This pattern has evolved historically, and never been consciously planned, although nearly all the written constitutions of Europe and Asia (excluding the Communist group) and also of Africa, have been drafted to conform with this evolutionary pattern in its most mature form. Real power is usually in the hands of the Prime Minister, if there is one, and if not it lies with the head of the state, either a King or a National leader, but much depends upon the personality of the men holding these offices, and they are always subject to control in varying degrees by the Council of Ministers, by the Parliament or by the Army.

The second group is American. It consists of a President, individual advisers and a legislature. Power is always vested in the President. Constitutions of this type are mostly to be found in North and South America, though where the United States has had predominent influence, as in Liberia and South Korea, this pattern has been followed. The restraining organ is the Congress, but in most American countries Congress has no power to overthrow a President in office, as the Parliaments of the Eurasian states have power to overthrow a constitutional Prime Minister and his Cabinet.

The third group consists of the Communist states. Even these today are becoming heterogeneous, though the basic pattern is the government of Soviet Russia. The written constitutions of these states provide for numerous presidencies, councils, chairmen, assemblies and other bodies, and it is difficult to identify the real seat of power, though the focal point is within the Communist party.

There is an objection to arraigning the head of a state before an international tribunal for a breach of International Law. Such proceedings would be offensive to the people collectively. In varying degrees people identify themselves with the personality of monarchs, or the heads of states, who, though not royal personages, have assumed, whether by election or revolution, whether indefinitely or for a term of years, the aura, though not the crown of kings.

The constitutions of forty-six of the present so-called independent sovereign states are of the Eurasian type, as against twenty-two of the American pattern and eleven Communist.[16] This reckoning ignores the miniature states and a dozen or so which are unclassifiable, though not of course unimportant.

This threefold classification is not intended to connote praise or criticism, nor does it correspond to the distinctions between monarchy and republicanism, or between democracy and dictatorship. There are dictatorships in all three groups, and the largest group, the Eurasian, contains both monarchies and republics. The purpose of making the classification is to examine whether any of these forms of government are constitutionally incompatible with the use of the proposed sanction of personal disqualification against the head of a state who may be responsible for a breach of international law. The problem lies in the nature of the functions of the head of the state. Wherever there is either a constitutional monarchy or a titular presidency there would be no difficulty because such a man could not be held responsible. The Prime Minister might in exceptional cases, for instance those involving local violence, be answerable internationally for his actions, and he could be declared *persona non grata* without attacking the constitutional functioning of an erring nation. Where the head of the state has real executive power however difficulties might arise. If a President were to order the use of physical violence against the people of another state in breach of international law, and were to be judged, whether or not he chose to defend himself, and found delinquent so that he would be liable to be disqualified from performing his international functions, then every international act performed by him, including the appointment of Ambassadors, would have to be treated as a legal nullity. Even if one could assume the willingness of most other states to apply the sanction, the result would be tantamount to boycotting the whole nation. Moreover, the propriety of a sanction directed against the head of a state might be widely doubted. It would offend against patriotic emotions which are still focussed upon Monarch or President. And this is especially true in the United States. The Americans who are by no means unduly respectful of men in high places, have a very strong and special regard for their President. These emotions would not be affected by a judgment against a Foreign Minister. For instance, if the American Secretary of State were to be condemned for delinquency in some hypothetical case, the judgment would carry some degree of conviction even to the people of the United States of America. These latter might very well support the policy of their own Secretary of State, but the judgment would not shock them. If, on the other hand the President were to be condemned and internationally repudiated, not only would the people of the United States be affronted, but the people of other countries not involved in the quarrel might sense a threat to their own Kings or Presidents, just as at the time of the French and Russian Revolutions the overthrow of monarchs was felt by the outside world to be an indirect threat to their own régimes. If an indirect threat were to be felt sufficiently strongly by peoples not involved in a quarrel, they could influence their own governments against applying the sanction to the President of the United States, and thus render ineffective the judgment of an International Court.

The focus of loyalty in all states today, whatever their constitutional form, and whatever political or economic doctrines they follow, is nationalistic. Any tendency towards internationalism, or any enforced interdependence, seems to be followed by an enthusiastic reaction in the direction of nationalism. The British felt an immense emotional relief after Dunkirk produced, apparently, by the knowledge that at last they were on their own, and no longer dependent upon allies, although they well knew that without American help they were doomed. The history of France ever since her rejection of the plan for a European Defence Community points the same way, in spite of many statesmen of international vision.

This emotional focus is personified by the head of the state. The question as to whether or not the head of a state should be subject to international judgment and liable to be penalised for an unlawful action thus poses the most difficult problem in the way of making international law effective by the method set out in this book, and the problem is not made any the easier by reason of the fact that the issue could not arise in matters affecting the majority of the Eurasian States, nor affecting Soviet Russia, for any state of any type may change its constitution, as France has done, and place at its head a strong ruler invested with executive authority.

If the rule of law over the nations is to be established however it cannot but be upon the principle enunciated traditionally by a Chief Justice of the Common Law of England, that the King ought not to be subject to any man, but to God and the Law. No constitutional ruler, certainly not the President of the United States, will quarrel with this dictum. No man, not even the head of a state, should be above the law.

There is therefore a conflict between logic and morals on the one hand and practicability on the other. The only way out of this dilemma is compromise. It is suggested that only in extremely grave cases should the conduct of a head of state be subject to judicial examination, and only then if there is no responsible minister, such as a Secretary of State for Foreign Affairs, who initiates and directs his country's international policy. Moreover where the head of a state is accused the Judges should limit themselves to giving a ruling on the law. They should not assess moral blame, and they should not recommend a penalty. These functions should be discharged politically by the Assembly of Nations, be it the General Assembly of the United Nations or the representatives of a group of nations acting together outside the framework of the Charter. A political Assembly could take into consideration all the consequences of boycotting the head of state, both psychological and economic, which judges could not do. Probably also the fear of an adverse legal judgment, even without penalty, would do much to control an executive president.

This solution, logically imperfect though it be, has the advantage of excluding from the operation of the sanction all democratically elected executive Presidents, and hereditary Kings who govern constitutionally, but it would not exclude the Heads of Police States, whose actions could be judicially examined from the point of view of international law, and who would risk bringing upon themselves and upon their people the inconvenient consequences of a collective boycott politically imposed. It is true that such a boycott might make a dictator an heroic figure among his own supporters at home, and even gather to him racial or ideological sympathisers outside the borders of his own land, but on the other hand a military dictator is not the focus of stable patriotic feelings, as is an elected president or hereditary monarch, and he must always contend with an underground opposition. The international action here proposed, partly legal and partly political would run no risk of making a man an international hero outside the field in which he were already an admired leader, and while not being in itself an inducement to the violent overthrow of a tyrant, it would rally the undecided or half-hearted to the support of the oppressed section of opinion.

9

The law to be applied

In proposing a definition of international delinquency, it has been stated that a breach of the rules of international law is an essential element of the offence. No attempt has been made to state what these rules are. For that, reference must be made to standard text books, and to writers of all nations on special subjects. There does not however exist any single authoritative work, nor any agreed body of doctrine to which a court of delinquency could be referred.

In November 1947 the General Assembly of the United Nations decided to establish an International Law Commission, whose task would be the promotion of the progressive development of international law [17] at least on certain subjects, with a view to the agreed codification of the law in accordance with Article 13, 1.a. of the Charter. This Commission has sat regularly for more than ten years, and has done a great deal of careful and detailed work which may ultimately be of real value, but which is only slowly achieving results because a restatement or codification of law is, if it is to be authoritative, an act tantamount to legislation, and no international legislature exists. If a restatement is to become authoritative, previous conflicting interpretations of doctrines or treaties would be made obsolete. It is manifest that international law is in need of this treatment, but no restatement or codification is at present possible, because the rights and duties of sovereign states cannot be altered, even by being redefined, without the individual consent of each state given at a diplomatic conference. This principle, which is of the essence of the existing system, is one of the few doctrines which are still universally held.

If however it is recognised that the declining sovereignty of nation states has undermined the existing system, to the extent that the state should no longer be regarded as the exclusively competent personality in international life, but that on the contrary it is a varied and changing succession of statesmen and officials who ought to be held answerable for breaches of international law, then new prospects appear.

There are several possibilities of advance, but all depend upon the existence of a court of international delinquency having authority to judge men for their official actions, and it would be premature to examine them until this proposal was well enough understood to have gained a large measure of acceptance. Broadly speaking the possibilities of legal development which present themselves, once this central idea is accepted, fall into two groups. If two-thirds of the members of the United Nations Assembly accept the proposal, and assert their competence to set up a judicial organ, then they would have to define what law the new court should apply in judging accused persons. In such case it would hardly depart from the description of international law set out by agreement for the Hague Court in Article 38 of its statute, which is annexed to the Charter.

The Article reads in part as follows:

'The Court ... shall apply:

a. International Conventions, whether general or particular, establishing rules expressly recognised by the contesting states;
b. International custom, as evidence of a general practice accepted as law;
c. The general principles of law recognised by civilised nations.
d. ... judicial decisions and the teachings of the most highly

qualified publicists of the various nations, as subsidiary means for the determination of rules of law.'

Though this clause has been criticised, it is the logical point of departure for any new court dealing with problems of international law. If the Assembly were to set up the new court, and to bear in mind the possibility of using the Hague Court as a final court of reference on points of law, it is obvious that the two courts should apply the same law. Only one adjustment would need to be made in adapting the words of paragraph a. of Article 38 in order to eliminate direct reference to the 'contesting states' in the statute of the new court and substitute for it a reference to the state on whose behalf an accused man had been officially acting.

If the court is to be open to litigants who are either companies incorporated under national law, or private persons, the law to be applied would have to include agreements between the collective or individual person on the one hand, and states or intergovernmental organizations on the other. This would extend the jurisdiction in some cases to the field of private international law, but as the line between public and private international law is by no means clearly drawn, there is no reason why this should not be done.

Legislative action is of two kinds. It can declare what the law is, or it can alter the law, either by amendment or by making new laws. The initial action of the Assembly should be merely declaratory. It would direct the new court to apply existing rules of law to individuals, and thus in certain circumstances stamp an action in breach of law as an offence, coming within the purview of the Court of Delinquency. Although the German and Japanese War Crimes trials may be perhaps considered as a useful political and psychological precedent for the proposal now made for the judgment and punishment of offenders by an international court, it is now essential to make an important legal distinction. The criticism that the London Agreement of the 8th August 1945, and the Charter annexed to it, created *ex post facto* criminal law insofar as it dealt with Crimes against the Peace and against Humanity, need not here be examined, as that part of the Nuremberg precedent obviously need not be followed. A much more technical objection was that according to international law no state may exercise jurisdiction over the official agents of another state without the consent of that state.[18]

This principle is known as the doctrine of act of state, and its usual operation is in time of peace to protect the official agent of one state from the jurisdiction of another state. It is an argument used to prevent domestic national courts from adjudicating on the officials actions of another sovereign state, done by its agents. Its application to the laws of war in a court established by many nations would give rise to objections which need not be discussed here, but as the doctrine could be used as an objection to the competence of the proposed court of delinquency, which is intended to operate in peace time, it is necessary to distinguish any international criminal jurisdiction, which either has been or may in the future be established, from the jurisdiction of the proposed court, in order that it may not be judged faulty on the ground of the act of state doctrine.[19]

No group of states, such as the signatories of the London Agreement could, it has been argued, exercise jurisdiction over German Statesmen, Generals and officials without the consent of a German government, which was, of course, not a signatory.

The reason a state may not exercise jurisdiction over the official agent of another state is that the act of the agent is the act of the state, and that the 'offending state,' being sovereign, is not subject to the domestic jurisdiction of the 'offended state.' One sovereign person cannot be subject to another sovereign person. From this proposition it might be argued that a group of 'offended states' ought not by agreement among themselves to bestow upon any court which they think it desirable to establish, the right to try and to punish the agents of an 'offending state,' even if they have power to enforce the judgment of the court. If the 'offended states,' by the instrumentality of their joint court, its judges and officials, prison officers and executioners, restrain the liberty and impose fines, imprisonment or death upon the agents of the 'offending state' they infringe the sovereignty of the latter, and thus act in breach of international law.

Although the sanction proposed in this book has been spoken of as a penalty in order to underline its sanctioning character, it is not in itself an action in breach of international law whereas the normal penalties of domestic criminal law mentioned above would be breaches of sovereignty if imposed upon the official agent of a foreign state. The new sanction is the exercise of a combined right and power which every state possesses by reason of its legal and its *de facto* sovereignty. The sanction will be imposed by the political decision of the law enforcing states, and not by the direct order of the Court of International Delinquency, whose jurisdiction, which need not even be initially termed a jurisdiction, will be merely to determine the legal issues, assess the blame, and recommend action to the law-enforcing states. It is not a breach of international law for a state or group of states to establish an organ composed of judges to advise it on law and recommend what action may be taken within the law to promote gradually a just and orderly regulation of world affairs.

As soon as the proposed Court or judicial organ were established, however, some reformulation of the law to be applied would be seen to be necessary in order to apply it to individuals.

As everyone who has handled international law knows, it is in a very unsatisfactory condition. Wherever the texts of international documents seemed to be insufficiently precise to be applied with certainty to individuals, other possibilities of legal development present themselves by reason of the fact that neither universal consent and in particular the consent of an 'offending state', nor the fiat of the veto powers, nor the cumbersome machinery of treaty making, would be required to establish the proposed system of personal responsibility for the giving of unprincipled international orders.

It is not proposed to alter the existing obligations of states, even by redefinition, in drafting the terms of reference of a Court of Delinquency. Clearer definitions of the duties of politicians would however sometimes be required. Known uncertainties in the law could thus be resolved beforehand, not *vis à vis* the states parties to an international agreement, but *vis à vis* the men who operate it, so that they would know how a court would interpret a given clause, and would know that, if accused of law breaking, they would not be able to rely upon an ambiguity construed in their favour to excuse them if the court were to consider their conduct blameworthy.

For instance, to take an extremely difficult issue by way of illustration, the Charter of the United Nations provides in Article 2 paragraph 4 that 'All members shall refrain in their international relations from the threat or use of force against the territorial integrity or political independence of any state ...' Article 51 provides that 'Nothing in the present Charter shall impair the inherent right of ... self-defence if an armed attack occurs against a member of the United Nations ...' These clauses are difficult, if not impossible, to apply to any particular outbreak of violence, in the absence of an authoritative definition of aggression. Attempts to formulate a definition have been made ever since the days of the League, but without success, partly because those who have worked on it have had to seek a form of words which would be almost universally acceptable, and in any case acceptable to the major military and economic powers.[20]

In the Assembly it has become almost a habit to vote in political blocs, because in deciding which way to vote on any given issue, each state considers future political alignments, rather than, or in any case as well as, the merits of the matter in hand. In seeking a definition of aggression the members of the United Nations have to consider how such a definition would affect them in some unspecified future conflict. Each state has in mind, not merely conflicts in which it may become directly engaged, but its relationships with economic or political allies which may be accused of aggression according to a definition. No government can afford to bind itself to take what might turn out to be the 'wrong' side, having regard to its current political necessities; that is to say, no state today will commit itself to take action against allied states. It would not be nearly so difficult to find a definition of aggression applicable to individuals, which would be applied, not by the Assembly but by a court in a concrete case, and which could not in any event engage a country to take military or economic measures against other states whose constant friendship and support are necessary to it.

A debate, the purpose of which is to produce universal agreement, takes a different course from a debate in which it is known beforehand that the vote of the majority will prevail, and a text resulting from the latter is much more lucid, because, where universal agreement is sought, concessions can be extracted by each member of a conference, every delegate knowing that if he makes a firm stand he can, single-handed, make the work of the conference abortive. The outcome of a debate on international delinquency would be to define the circumstances in which a principal executive, Prime Minister or other public servant, could be held personally to blame for the threat or use of violence, though the legal responsibility of his country would not be affected. As however the legal responsibility of a state for an act of violence is seldom the subject of a court judgment, and then only, as in the case of the Corfu Channel, in terms of money damages which cannot be enforced, the legal position of the state concerned is relatively unimportant.

The definition of aggression is an ambitious example, and no doubt it would be necessary to proceed conservatively, especially if the plan were to be put into operation by the Assembly of the United Nations. Use could be made of the work of the International Law Commission, whose work has so far made little impression on account of the over-riding necessity of universal agreement, and of the practice of bloc voting in the Assembly.

The advantage of acting through the United Nations if this can be achieved is that it would secure the continuity of legal authority, and thus the confidence of the population of the world in the truly legal character of the new court and its judgments. Such confidence is the real root of law. If however, the requisite two-thirds majority were not forthcoming, or if there were an adverse advisory opinion from the Hague as to the powers of the Assembly, there would still be no impediment to independent action by a group of states. No one doubts that as far as law enforcement goes, we are still, internationally, in the age of self-help. In a limited way the North Atlantic Treaty Organisation is an example of this. Failing any hope of agreement in the Security Council, and recognising that that body was incapable of maintaining world security, which is its primary task, the original members of NATO made what is in form a treaty, but in substance a joint declaration, that they proposed to make common plans to deal with certain dangers to the peace.

Similarly, if a substantial body of nations were to come to the conclusion that any breach of international law is, if not subject to penalties, a potential danger to them because lawless behaviour is dangerous to any community, there would be nothing in the Charter of the United Nations, nor in general or particular international law, to prevent them from making a joint declaration that, their own safety being endangered by the increasing lawlessness of all nations, they proposed to declare delinquent, in accordance with the judgment of a court, any individual found to be to blame for a breach of international law wherever committed, with the consequence that the law-breaker would henceforward be treated as *persona non grata* within all their territories. Such action is within their existing rights. All that would be needed would be joint action taken as the result of a recommendation of independent and impartial professional judges. The judicial machinery would be set up by them, but neither the judges nor the administrative staff would need to be chosen exclusively from among their own nationals.

Such a body of law-enforcing states would not necessarily be tied to the description of international law set out in Article 38 of the Statute of the Hague Court, since it would not be entitled to use that Court as a final Court of Reference on points of law. This great loss might however be balanced by the fact that there would be greater liberty to select, redefine and even codify those parts of the existing body of international law, which are relevant to the immediate needs of the world. A great deal of law found today in text books is obsolete, owing to the rapid technical advance of our generation. Maritime law, for instance, including the law governing the maritime belt, has developed since the days of sailing ships, and has an archaic texture, and the law of the air, though it dates only from the Warsaw Convention of 1925, is not capable of governing excursions into space.

A very long digression would be needed to examine the laws of war, and it must suffice here to say that with the coming of nuclear weapons, those conventional rules which governed the conduct of warfare, and were dependent upon making a distinction between military forces and civilians, have become unreal. It must also be admitted that not only would the sanction not be strong enough to control the behaviour of men, either military or civilian, in wartime, but it could not prevent a government from resorting to war if its members believed there was grave danger of attack from other states. Neither law, nor any human power, can control a state which possesses modern weapons and becomes involved in war, and the law-enforcing states would do well to admit this at the outset. This is not by any means to say the nuclear experiments, and the construction of nuclear weapons, could not ultimately be controlled by the system of judgment and sanctions here proposed, but the system would have to be well established upon a basis of world-wide public opinion before any attempt could be successfully made to outlaw them. World opinion is, no doubt, opposed to the testing, manufacture and use of nuclear weapons, as it is in a general way opposed to all out-breaks of violence, but there is as yet no channel for the effective co-ordination and expression of such feelings. The policy here proposed would supply such a channel, but what is perhaps of more immediate importance, it would supply a channel for the expression of public indignation against foreign politicians. In national law it is necessary to have strong criminal law which matches in severity the general anger at certain types of crime, because if offenders are insufficiently punished, public feeling will show itself in uncontrolled outbursts of mob violence and lynchings. There is at present no international channel of this kind, so that resentment accumulates to flashpoint and issues in war.

The sanction will not be complete until a man is repudiated by his own people. This can scarcely happen in our generation. National sentiment is very strong in all countries. Support within a nation for an adverse international judgment, apart from political party manoeuvres, is far in the future, and even if it were fairly strong it could not overthrow a dictatorship. Such regimes are however even now sensitive to world opinion, and seek either to conceal their worst excesses or else to justify them at the bar of world opinion. International pressure could therefore be brought upon them to conform, even in their internal affairs, with minimum standards of justice. Once the practice of judging and punishing delinquent individuals were widely accepted, the law-enforcing states could from time to time make declarations to the effect that certain defined actions, such for instance as actions conflicting with the Universal Declaration of Human Rights, would henceforward be treated as delinquent.

That purely declaratory document is not now part of international law, because the draft covenants intended to be binding have not yet been agreed by the negotiating states, though they have been under discussion for many years. Moreover, the document itself is expressed as a statement of principles, rather than a definition of obligations, and it could therefore only be treated as a basis for selective directions to the court of delinquency. It is however in common use in the Secretariats of the United Nations and other international agencies, whenever these are called upon to advise the Trusteeship Council, or other executive councils, as to what, if any, action may be taken as the result of individual petitions from persons or groups aggrieved by the treatment they have received at the hands of their own governments. To this very limited extent it has a certain status in international law even today. Moreover it has formed the basis of a Convention for the protection of human rights [21] recently agreed by a number of European states which have established a Commission and a Court to deal with claims, though this convention and the organs thereby established operate only within the territory of the concurring states. The Commission may, according to Article 25 'receive petitions addressed to the Secretary General of the Council of Europe from any person, non-governmental organisation, or group of individuals claiming to be the victim of a violation by one of the High Contracting Parties of the rights set forth in (the) Convention,' subject to certain conditions. The new European Convention thus bestows rights arising under international law directly upon individuals. The recommendation made in this book that individuals should be made personally responsible under international law for breaches of its obligations, is not therefore without logical precedent. The only attempts so far made to hold individuals responsible for disregarding, such obligations have been the war crimes trials during the 20th century, and the abortive drafts of the International Law Commission for an international criminal code. Neither war crimes trials, nor an agreed criminal code, can however guarantee security, or lay the foundations of the rule of law.

They depend upon military victory by whichever side is presupposed to be in the right, as judged by its own political leaders, for military action cannot await a Court Judgment. Such measures cannot therefore fulfil the primary purpose of a sanction, which is the certainty of incurring a penalty in case of illegal action.

The organised exclusion of men in official positions from international society when their conduct has been impartially judged to have been illegal could operate as a sanction inside the existing system of international law. It could be applied only to the servants and representatives of those states which, by an international convention, have given preliminary consent to the plan. There is however no legal necessity so to limit its application. There is no legal impediment in the way of a state, and in particular a group of states, which may decide to refuse recognition to any foreign statesman of any nation, and to deny him access to their territory. Sovereign states have this right and this power if the conduct of the man in question is politically distasteful to them. They are not obliged by existing law to recognise and receive any foreign citizen whatever position he may hold in his home country. They can reject him even if no judges have ruled that his policy has been executed by unlawful means. It follows that this penalty could be applied politically outside the field of existing international rules of behaviour. Its efficacy in controlling the actions of international statesmen depends however upon the number of participating states, and upon the extent to which they can command the support of world opinion.

Even in this century, when respect for international law by governments has reached its nadir, the concept of legality and the hope, or dream, that by some device, some change of heart, some cession of sovereignty to a central authority, world affairs may come to be regulated in an orderly and rational manner are very much alive in men's minds. Respect for the existing rules of international law is the only safe point of departure even though they be incomplete and unsatisfactory. If the sanction proposed were to be used for purely political ends by a group of states bound together by an ideology, and exercising great economic and military influence in the world, the plan would fail, for it would become a battlecry of political partizans. All systems of law, even the very best, are capable of misuse, sometimes with the best intentions, and in the end the only safeguard is the character of the men who administer them. It is easy to see how a large group of powerful states, for instance the Western allies, organized as they are in a defensive alliance, might with the best will in the world, collectively impose this new sanction in cases of misbehaviour by communist rulers, when force was inappropriate or dangerous. This would serve no good purpose. It would indeed bring the law into contempt. The only safeguard against such misuse is the impartiality of the men called to judge international issues. They must be impartial in national origin and in personal character. If such men can be found the system can work and develop and their existence will guard against its misuse, for if a panel of impartial judges were to be established no attempt to use the sanction irregularly for ideological purposes would command respect. If, however the existing rules of international law were taken as a basis, and if the notion of *mens rea* were introduced into the instructions initially given to the Judges, then their judgment or recommendation, and the collective action taken in consequence thereof by the law-enforcing states, could command the assent of world opinion.

Because the sanction can operate freely in accordance with the existing rules of international law, and yet its operation is not technically restricted to the consensual framework within which those rules have been formulated, the proposed plan would work slowly as a solvent agent for combining the discordant elements of law and sovereignty. The nation states, new and old, would retain their sovereignty for so long as they desired to do so. They would remain the law makers by exercising their present treaty-making power within the existing framework of international thought, but so soon as it was perceived that by shifting the focus of international obligation from the collective national 'person,' which the sovereign has now become, to the individual who is in fact responsible, the nation states would discover that they already have the power not only to secure obedience to the imperfect law of today, but to develop it and resolve its contradictions. International law is weak because it is not enforced. It is not enforced because it is defective, and because the sanctions so far proposed for its enforcement are too costly and too dangerous. Economic and military sanctions may possibly be used in case of unbearable necessity, in the secondary sense of the word sanction, that is to say to correct a breach of law after it has been committed. They do not, and never can come into play in the primary sense every time a policy of dubious legality is under discussion. The new sanction of personal disgrace and exclusion from the honour and prestige of international work would operate constantly in the primary sense thus bringing the men who are occupied with world affairs by a slow educational process to an acceptance of their international responsibilities.

Appendix

In order not to interrupt the presentation of the idea contained in this book no attempt has been made to intersperse the text with illustrations of its possible effect in practice were it to be adopted as a policy and carried out by a majority of states. In this appendix it is intended to take certain international incidents which have happened since the end of World War II and consider briefly what the effect a Court of International Delinquency could have had upon events had it been in existence at the time of these various incidents and to indicate who would have been the proper defendants. Such a proceeding is necessarily speculative for it is impossible to turn back the pages of history and say with certainty what would have happened had a factor been present which was lacking at the time. It is emphatically not suggested that a new Court should be given *ex post facto* jurisdiction, even though some of the episodes to be examined present continuing problems. The future conduct of responsible rulers and officials should alone come within the new jurisdiction.

The Berlin Blockade There was no formal agreement between the Russian Authorities on the one hand and the American, British and French on the other, covering the right of surface transport between the Western Zones of Germany and the Western Sectors of Berlin. Consequently every journey by road or rail across the Russian Zone was by permission and passengers were subject to documentary examinations, which varied in their thoroughness, at Russian check points on entering and leaving the Russian Zone. Increasing friction between the Western and Russian authorities at the Control Council and its subordinate committees, and failure to agree on a number of topics proposed for joint policy action was accompanied by increasing Russian suspicions. The Russians alleged that the Western Commanders were using their transit trains to evacuate Germans from Russian jurisdiction in their Sector and Zone. These suspicions led to prolonged delays on the railways and to corresponding irritation and mutual distrust.

One of the main subjects of disagreement in the Control Council had been currency reform. The Reichsmark was a valueless currency and dealings great and small were either in real goods or speculative values. New money was vital to Germany as a whole. Failing agreement at the Control Council the Western Military Governors produced at great speed the Western Deutsche-Mark for their three Zones and overnight the empty shops were filled with consumer goods. The new money commanded confidence and a further decision was taken to introduce it into the Western Sectors of Berlin. The Russians declared that this would create a black market in currency in Berlin and sealed off their Sector and their Zone. They continued to respect the only explicit transit agreement binding upon them covering the air corridors. The airlift was a tremendous technical success. The facts leading up to the blockade were not publicised in America or Britain and the consequent emotional tension produced the iron curtain as we know it today. Pride in the airlift and in the economic sunrise in western Germany and resentment at Russian intransigeance filled the minds of the western peoples. Anger at what they believed to be western trickery in misusing military trains for political purposes and in endangering their precarious economic control of eastern Germany by introducing the new currency into Berlin filled the minds of the Russians. This dangerous tension was only resolved because in 1949 neither side had recovered from the effects of the World War. They were in no state to embark upon another.

Had a Court of Deliquency been in existence the Russians would have been able to air their grievances through a defined legal channel instead of by clumsy and damaging political expedients. They could have alleged that the Western Commanders were abusing their privilege of military transport and that in introducing the new currency they were breaking the agreement of June 5th, 1945. There might very well not have been enough evidence for a Court to adjudicate upon the first ground of complaint, and on the second there was a substantial degree of economic justification. It would be altogether too speculative to attempt a judgement now, but if there had been a court which could have judged the issues, an impartial statement of the facts, in so far as they were ascertainable, would have done much to clarify the minds of people who saw the whole episode through the restrictive and emotionally distorted spectacles imposed by their own political allegiances. Finally, however, it may be said with certainty that if those responsible for making the arrangements which divided Germany and Berlin had known at the time that they or their colleagues might one day be called personally to account for their actions they would have been a great deal more careful to define their rights and obligations beforehand, for a *causa sine qua non* of the blockade was the lack of precise agreement on the surface transit arrangements between the Western Zones and the Western Sectors. The problems arising out of this failure still present danger to the world.

The proper defendants would have been the British and American Zone Commanders if the Russians had brought an accusation, the Russian Zone Commander, if the Western Allies had brought a counter suit. It would have been unnecessary and undesirable to bring in the Western foreign ministers.

'Mc Carthyism' in the United Nations and its Agencies The interrogatory procedures associated with the name of Senator McCarthy were not confined to officials of the United States Government and employees of American institutions. They were also directed to a number of American citizens who were International Civil Servants in the employment of the United Nations and its Specialised Agencies. The United States Government demanded the dismissal of those International Officials who failed to satisfy the Interrogating Boards that they were free of Communist associations. The demand was, in the case of one organization, followed by a threat that if the Executive Head of this International Organization did not comply with the request of the United States Government the latter would withdraw its support from the Organisation concerned.[22] This demand was contrary to Article 100 paragraph 2 of the Charter and to the Constitutions of the Agencies whereby member nations undertook not to seek to influence the Executive Heads in the discharge of their responsibilities. The Executive Heads, however, for the most part complied with the American demands under pressure. The International Officials resorted to such Administrative Tribunals as were open to them demanding reinstatement by the Organisation which had employed them, or else compensation. A large proportion were awarded compensation but were not reinstated. Some failed by reason of the temporary character of their contracts. Had they been able to avail themselves of a Court of International Delinquency the results might have been very different. The Executive Heads who yielded to American governmental pressure did so only after prolonged struggles. To comply with the American request was contrary to Article 100 paragraph 1 of the Charter which forbade them to receive instructions from any government, and which applied to them all. Had they been subject to judgement by a Court of Delinquency they could have replied to American pressure that the course of action required of them would have been a violation of the Charter and might

result in their own loss of office. A Secretary General or Director General of an International Organisation judged delinquent by a panel of impartial judges could scarcely maintain his position before the world, and were a large majority of the members of the United Nations to establish such a court it can be assumed that they would apply the penalty of international ostracism suggested in this book. The existence of the Court proposed would therefore be a weapon in the hands of the Secretary General and of the other heads of agencies in case of national pressure brought to bear upon them.

Officials of the American State Department who exercised the pressure in these cases would themselves have been answerable to a Court of Delinquency and this factor might very well have restrained them, in so far as their international policy was concerned. For them also the existence of the Court would have been a means of defence against the attack of the Senator. In so far as Senator McCarthy was responsible for this unhappy chapter in the history of the United Nations and its Agencies, he could himself have been judged delinquent and this might well have terminated his influence long before the Senate itself took action against him.

The proper defendants would have been the Secretary General of the United Nations, the Directors General of the Specialized Agencies concerned, officials of the State Department, the United States permanent delegates, and Senator McCarthy himself.

The Nationalisation of the Suez Canal. July 1956 Nationalisation was carried out abruptly and caused great indignation in many interested countries, notably the United Kingdom and France. Colonel Nasser was widely accused of breach of treaty. All through the summer and early autumn of that year political discussion continued in London and Paris. Various devices were adumbrated for compelling or inducing Colonel Nasser to respect the rights of nations which used the canal. It was genuinely feared that the Egyptians would not be capable of managing the canal. The British and French Governments took the line that international obligations must be respected. The matter could have been referred to the Hague Court had the contending governments been willing to take this course. No move however was made in this direction, either because there was no compulsory jurisdiction, or because of the delays involved, or because the aggrieved governments feared that they had no certainty of winning. Isolated voices were raised in England declaring that Colonel Nasser was no more guilty of illegal action than were those who nationalised or confiscated privately owned industries in many other countries either side of the iron curtain. These comparisons were not always apt, but the legal issue was clouded in the minds of those peoples who had a national interest in the free navigation of the canal. Colonel Nasser was presented in the press as the butt of the cartoonists and the violator of international engagements. Had a court of International Delinquency existed the proper complainant would have been the Suez Canal Company itself rather than the governments claiming under breach of treaty. It was the Company and its shareholders who were immediately wronged by the act of nationalisation, supposing it to have been illegal, and they ought to have had the primary right to decide as to whether or not to litigate subject to the control of an international parquet as described in this book. Had this been possible the political tension would necessarily have been held in check pending litigation, and the legal issues would thus have been clarified. As things are the question as to whether or not the act of nationalisation was illegal remains a matter of opinion very much subordinated to political emotion. Had the legal issue been decided one way of the other the consequences would certainly have been different. Had it been established that Colonel Nasser had the right to do what he did the user countries would have been confined to free and equal negotiation unmixed with threats and abuse, and had the case gone the other way the offended states would have had the support of world opinion in any political or even military action they might have thought proper to take.

The proper defendant, having regard to local political conditions, was Colonel Nasser, not his foreign minister.

The Israeli invasion of Sinai and the Franco-British intervention in Egypt October and November 1956 The Israeli invasion was not provoked by the nationalisation of the canal but by Arab encirclement, frontier raids on both sides, and the continuing refusal of the Egyptians to permit Israel to use the Canal. It is not possible to say whether or not Israel received any promises of active or passive support from France or Great Britain. Therefore the possibility of collusion or connivance will not be dealt with here except to say that had a Court of Delinquency been in existence these questions would have been germane to its deliberations after the events of that autumn. Israel's complaints against Egypt by reason of the latter's refusal of free passage for Israeli ships and cargoes could have been made the subject of a delinquency suit long before 1956. The abortive resolutions of the United Nations could not have the psychological effect of an independent judgement and the application of the proposed sanction to Colonel Nasser. It must be emphasized that rulers in positions of dictatorial power are very often helplessly subject to the passions of the people whom they rule. Colonel Nasser could not have maintained his position in Egypt if he had voluntarily yielded to rights claimed by Israel. Had he been faced squarely with a choice between international outlawry and obedience to the law he might well have found it politically expedient to yield. This is speculation. The power of the proposed sanction can only be discovered by trial, but it may well operate as an aid to rulers such as Colonel Nasser who, in weighing the pros and cons, dare not at present choose the path of legality for fear of their extremist supporters.

Because the legality or otherwise of the nationalization of

the canal was never tested, the policy of Great Britain and France during the succeeding months was based upon the assumption that Colonel Nasser had broken the law. Negotiations led nowhere, and the United Nations was powerless. In the circumstances the French and British leaders believed themselves to be entitled to protect the interests of their own countries by all available means. Throughout the negotiations with Colonel Nasser the threat of force had lurked in the background, thus making it more difficult for him to come to terms with them.[20] The legality of the ultimatum of October 1956 and of its consequences was evidently not considered seriously by Sir Anthony Eden, for when he was asked in the House of Commons whether Great Britain was at war with Egypt and whether the Prisoners of War Convention would apply to captured British troops it was manifest that he had not taken detailed advice as to the legal position of his country. The sitting was suspended for half an hour owing to the unmanageable conduct of the opposition, and this permitted time for hasty legal consultation among other more urgent discussions. When the sitting was resumed Sir Anthony had been primed with a legal answer. He said that there was a state of armed conflict between Great Britain and Egypt and that the Convention would be applied even though it had not been ratified. The existence of a Court of Delinquency prior to the nationalization of the canal would, as has been said, have affected the whole course of the negotiations between July and October of that year, but it would also have had the effect of causing the British Prime Minister to take legal advice quietly before he made a decision, rather than in the heat of a parliamentary debate. In any society governed by law responsible people take legal advice before they decide what to do. The absence in 1956 of any Court capable of judging the conduct of statesmen produced a situation in which the British Government declared itself to be acting in defence of international legal obligations, the content of which it itself judged, and yet it failed to take any sufficient legal advice as to its own legal rights and duties before embarking upon military action.

Colonel Nasser would have been the proper defendant to an Israeli suit regarding the closing of the Canal to Israeli ships and cargoes. Mr. Ben Gurion was responsible for the Sinai invasion. The Prime Ministers and Foreign Secretaries of Britain and France should have been made defendants in respect of the intervention in Egypt. It is admitted that the sanction could not have controlled Mr. Ben Gurion, but submitted that the threat of it might well have controlled the British Ministers and through them the French.

The Russian intervention in Hungary in October and November 1956

What discussions took place within the Kremlin before it was decided to intervene in Hungary and overthrow the emergent and antisoviet regime are not publicly recorded. The care taken by the Russians to ensure that their government was invited to intervene shows however that formal legal requirements were not ignored. The whole Soviet record since the second world war displays a policy of compliance with the strict forms of legal engagement as witness the respect for the agreement covering the air corridors during the Berlin Blockade. The legality or otherwise of the intervention in Hungary depends entirely upon whether or not the Kadar Government was the lawful government at the time it issued its request for help to the Russians. If it was, then the Russian intervention was no more illegal than the landing of American troops in the Lebanon some two years later in response to a request from the Lebanese government. Whether a given régime is a lawful one or not, depends upon a number of factors both internal and external to the country. The Kadar government was not however in command of the country and could not have gained control without Soviet intervention. The legality of the Russian move was therefore dubious, to say the least, even though before a court of law they would have had a colourable argument. No doubt the

Russian decision was taken on political grounds, but though nothing is known for certain it is the common opinion in the West that it was preceded by long debates. Since some legal aspects of the action were certainly considered, the existence of a Court of Delinquency which might have been charged with the duty of examining their conduct would have focussed the minds of those who favoured intervention upon the legal factor, and might perhaps have tipped the scale. More than this cannot be said.

The real Ruler for the time being – Mr. Kruschev – would have been the proper defendant.

The territory of South West Africa and the colour issue In the administration of justice within a state it is very often necessary to take proceedings against a misdemeanant in respect of some only of his actions which are known or suspected to be illegal, either because evidence is lacking to prove criminal guilt, or because the law does not cover the whole field of socially objectionable conduct.

The treatment of dark-skinned people by the Union of South Africa since the end of the second World war has profoundly disturbed the world. It has become a matter of international interest and importance inasmuch as continuing racial tension seems likely to provoke violence which would not necessarily be confined to the Union of South Africa. It could spread to the whole continent and beyond. Nevertheless the only internationally delinquent action with which the men responsible for the policy of apartheid can at present be charged is in relation to the territory of South West Africa. This territory, originally a German Colony, was made a mandate under the League of Nations between the wars. After the liquidation of the League the mandated territories were for the most part transformed into Trust Territories under Chapter XII of the Charter of the United Nations. The Union of South Africa, which was the administering power in the days of the League, not only did not take this step but also refused in the face of a succession of United Nations resolutions to take the actions required under Article 73 of the Charter in respect of non-self-governing territories. An advisory opinion of the Hague Court requested by the United Nations in 1950 recommended that the territory of South West Africa should be registered as a Trust Territory but the majority of the Court was unable to rule that there was a legal obligation on the Union to do so. The United Nations Assembly set up a sub-committee to deal with the problem but has made no effective progress in safeguarding the rights of the population of the territory. The subcommittee somewhat naturally aims at securing the highest possible degree of supervision over this territory by inducing the Union of South Africa to deal with it as a Trust. Politically this is a reasonable course, but it would be better to handle it as a legal issue and, if the responsible ministers in the Union Government could be accused of internationally delinquent conduct in respect of the minimum legal obligations incumbant upon the government, there can be no doubt that in the present state of world opinion a judicial recommendation that they should be excluded from international society would be widely implemented.

A boycott on South African exports was organised in the United Kingdom in 1960 as a protest against the apartheid policy, and there have been many privately directed campaigns whose object was to bring outside opinion to bear upon the Government of the Union. These campaigns have probably had some temporary effect at least upon the business community of South Africa, and thus indirectly upon the Government, but there has been no change of policy. The general condemnation of that policy is unlikely to have any effect unless it can be focussed upon the responsible men through a legal channel, and this cannot be done until machinery exists for judging them upon issues which are justiciable. Merely to pass resolutions and make declarations to the effect that their conduct is inhumane and dangerous will lead nowhere. Succeeding administrations in South Africa have shown themselves to be sensitive to legal forms even while their policies appear to be in conflict with principles which are enshrined within the Anglo-Saxon concept of the rule of law. It took them five years of constitutional manoevering to amend the franchise laws affecting the coloured people in the Cape Province, and they were careful for many years to maintain a limited observance of the law laid down in the Hague Advisory Opinion relating to the territory of South West Africa. If they have now trespassed beyond the terms of the Charter of the United Nations in their administration of that territory it is partly due to the absence of any legal channel whereby the undoubted force of world opinion could be brought to bear upon them personally. It is of course impossible to be certain that the method of judgement and sanction proposed in this book would be strong enough to compel the South African statesmen to obey the rules of international law. The fear of the white men surrounded by black men who outnumber them may prove uncontrollable, and if this is so the colour problem is a survival problem and cannot be resolved by legal procedure. A clear definition of the rights and wrongs of the matter would however do much to prevent the conflict from spreading.

All ministers from time to time whose departmental responsibilities have included the Territory of South West Africa would have been and would be proper defendants.

Tibet The Peking government of China has been accused of internationally unlawful conduct chiefly in connection with the occupation of Tibet and its treatment of the inhabitants. American influence has so far excluded the Peking government from the United Nations. This exclusion does not absolve it from compliance with the rules of international law. Nevertheless to exclude a government from the principal forum of world affairs and at the same time to expect it to conform itself to the standards which are being developed in that forum is illogical. The mainland of China is treated as an outlaw state. How then demand from it obedience to the law? The rational course is to bring it in and then bring pressure to bear upon it to behave lawfully by means of the procedure proposed in this book. This procedure can be applied whether or not a government has agreed to it. Once the Peking government is bound by the terms of the Charter on points of substance, the machinery of law enforcement which has been described would be applicable to the effective rulers of China whether or not they had participated in its establishment.

Here the defendant would be the effective ruler of China.

The U.2. episode and the Summit Conference 1960 An American aeroplane – the U 2 – was brought down on Russian territory in circumstances which left little doubt that the pilot was engaged in espionage by photographing Russian installations. This was later acknowledged by the President of the United States. The consequence was the abandonment of the proposed Summit Conference of May 1960 by the refusal of the Russians to take part except under politically impossible conditions. The proposals made in this book provide a remedy for just such a situation.

The Russians demanded an apology for breach of Sovereignty, and punishment of the men responsible. In the setting of the twentieth century war of ideas the head of the greatest western state felt unable to accede to this demand. Had the Russians been able to avail themselves of the legal procedure suggested in this book, the emotions which led them to torpedo the Summit Conference would have been siphoned into a legally defined channel. Their indignation would have been directed to the man responsible – the head of the American Intelligence Services, who would have been made defendant in a suit of international delinquency and, if judged guilty of wilfully committing a breach of international law, would have been penalised by the condemnation of a court of independent judges and by future exclusion from international society.

It may be that this would not have hurt him very much, as he may not care to travel widely nor aspire to any office from which such a sentence would exclude him. Nevertheless, even the possibility of such a proceeding would have had certain consequences both for the Americans and the Russians. With the possibility of a legal remedy available to them and, as must be admitted, every hope of winning before the Court, the Russians could have made no propaganda move at a political or diplomatic level, save perhaps a demand to postpone the Summit, pending the determination of the legal issue. Had they anticipated the Court's decision by diplomatic intransigeance they would have put themselves in the wrong before the world. It may be true that Mr. Kruschev was acting in Paris against his own best judgment and under pressure from sections of his own people – the Party and the Army – but the leverage exercised by these upon him would have been deprived of force if legal proceedings had been available. The condemnation of a responsible official by an international court could be regarded by the Russians as a more telling humiliation for the United States than any presidential apology, and the demand for the punishment of the offenders would have been met.

The allegation that it was Mr. Kruschev's intention to wreck the summit in any event is not borne out by his immediate reactions to the U 2 episode, and even if rigorist party members and Red Army generals had this intention all along, they could not have used the U 2 disaster to enforce their wishes had proper legal redress been available.

On the American side it was recognised that the conventions of nineteenth century diplomacy are no longer realistic, and therefore they acknowledged their spy. Wise or foolish, this action would have been irrelevant had the system of international delinquency proposed in this book been in operation, for the Russians would have been as free as any other complainant to choose their defendant or defendants. Mr. Kruschev was probably right in thinking that this particular flight was not specifically authorised at a higher political level, and this early admission would very likely have been sufficient to cause a court to exonerate all senior holders of public office in the United States from deliberate complicity in that particular breach of Russian sovereignty. Moreover, in the course of a judicial hearing the allegations of spying by the Russians in the American Embassy in Moscow, and in the territory of the United States could have been presented and sifted in justification of the American spying operations over Russian territory. Once these arguments and counter arguments had been impartially judged the way would have been open for summit negotiations.

As it appeared from newspaper reports that the decision to make the flight was not taken at a high political level, the proper defendant would have been the head of the intelligence service. The legal judgment would have redressed the situation even though the penalty might not have harmed him greatly.

Possibly, however, the new President might have found it politic to appoint another head of intelligence and would thus have received different and perhaps better informed advice touching the affair of Cuba in 1961.

Notes and References

1. There are exceptions to this general rule. For instance 'a pirate and his vessel lose *ipso facto* by an act of piracy the protection of their flag state, and their national character. Every maritime state has, by customary rule of the law of nations, the right to punish pirates. And the vessels of all nations, whether men-of-war, other public vessels, or merchantmen, can on the open sea chase, attack and seize the pirate, and bring him home for trial and punishment by the courts of their own country.' Oppenheim's *International law*: Lauterpacht, Vol. 1. 8th ed. p. 616. Moreover those accused of offences against the laws of war who fall into the hands of the enemy can in certain conditions be tried before the termination of hostilities (*op. cit.*, Vol. II, pp. 390–391). Thus jurisdiction over the individual citizen of a foreign state can in exceptional cases be exercised in war time without the consent of that state and without awaiting its submission induced by military defeat.

2. See Oppenheim, *op. cit.*, Vol. II, p. 219: '... a peace treaty imposed by a victorious aggressor has no legal validity, notwithstanding the rule that international law disregards the vitiating effect of duress.' The difficulty of defining aggression is however so well known that at present the legal validity of a peace treaty would seem to depend upon a political rather than a legal judgment.

3. Cf. the establishment of a Military Commission and the

Council of War by order of General Scott at Tampico on the 19th February 1847. See N. Winthrop, *Military Law and Precedents*. 2nd ed., p. 839. Washington, Government Printing Office 1920. See also Oppenheim, *op. cit.*, Vol. II, p. 612, from which it appears that the right to try persons accused of war crimes exists unless waived by the Peace Treaty which is considered to waive all claims whether or not it contains an amnesty clause. See also A. Mérignac, 'De la sanction des infractions du droit des gens,' *Revue Générale de droit international public*, Tome XXIV, Paris 1917, p. 5 ff.

4. See Resolution 489 (V), 12th December 1950 of the General Assembly of the United Nations. See also General Assembly, Official Records, 7th Session. Supplement No 11 (A/2136) and 9th Session. Supplement No 12 (A/2645).

5. This weakness was not recognized by the draftsmen of the Covenant of the League of Nations. Article 10 of the Covenant provides that 'The Members of the League undertake to respect and preserve *as against external aggression* the territorial integrity and political independence of all Members of the League,' but Article 16 provides that 'should any Member of the League Resort to war in disregard of its covenants ... it shall *ipso facto* be deemed to have committed an act of war against all other Members of the League'. Provisions for international "sanctions" then follow. See also H. C. Nicholas, *The United Nations as a political institution*, O.U.P. (1959), p. 64: 'The core of the Security Council plan lay in the assumption of Great Power Unity. The wars it was to stop were conflicts among other Powers ...'

6. It is true that Article 1 of the United Nations Charter states that the purposes are: '1. to maintain international peace ...' but it is submitted that a just ordering of world affairs ought to be the paramount aim and that peace is merely the desirable consequence of that achievement.

7. Blake, *Gnomic verses*. XVII, 1.

8. Shelley, *Prometheus Unbound*, ll. 573–4.

9. Article 34, paragraph 1 of the Statute of the International Court of Justice.
10. Kolrausch-Lange, *Strafgesetzbuch*, 39 and 40, Auflage III.
11. Archbold, *Criminal Pleading*, 29th ed., p. 692.
12. Derry v. Peek 14 A.C. 337 at p. 374.
13. Hans Kelsen, *The Law of the United Nations*, Stevens, 2nd impression 1951, p. 489.
14. The suggestion that an international Parquet should be established was made by several contributors in the reports on the punishment of war crimes at the London International Assembly during World War II.
15. Records of the General Conference of Unesco, Second Extraordinary Session, Paris 1953 III 4 (88).
16. This classification is based on information published in standard works of reference and is necessarily out of date. Existing states have changed their real constitutional nature and new states have come into being.
17. Article 1 of the Statute of the Commission.
18. Hans Kelsen, 'Will the Nuremberg Trial Constitute a Precedent?,' *The International Law Quarterly*, Vol. I, No 2, 1947.
19. The definition of this doctrine given by Oppenheim, *op. cit.*, Vol. I, p. 267, is as follows: 'A consequence of equality – or independence – of states is that the courts of one state do not as a rule, question the validity or legality of the official acts of another sovereign state or the official or officially avowed acts of its agents, at any rate insofar as those acts purport to take effect within the sphere of the latter state's jurisdiction.
20. There are may other reasons. See Julius Stone, *Aggression and World Order*, Stevens 1958.
21. Convention for the protection of Human Rights and Fundamental Freedoms, signed at Rome on the 4th November 1950.
22. Records of the General Conference of Unesco. Second Extraordinary Session. Paris 1953, 2 XC/7, p. 2.

Index

For headings not appearing in the index consult the Table of Contents.

GPSR Compliance

The European Union's (EU) General Product Safety Regulation (GPSR) is a set of rules that requires consumer products to be safe and our obligations to ensure this.

If you have any concerns about our products, you can contact us on ProductSafety@springernature.com

In case Publisher is established outside the EU, the EU authorized representative is:

Springer Nature Customer Service Center GmbH
Europaplatz 3
69115 Heidelberg, Germany

Batch number: 10822832

Printed by Printforce, the Netherlands